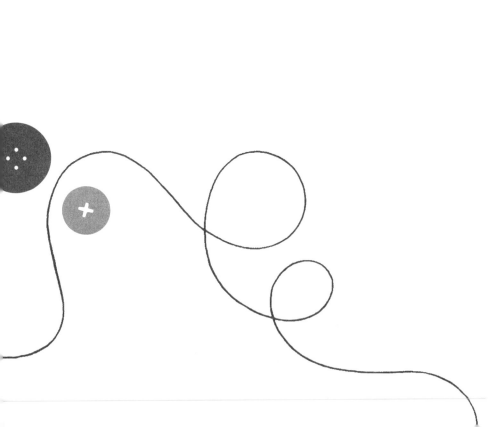

Craft INC.

Turn Your Creative Hobby Into a Business

Meg Mateo Ilasco

CHRONICLE BOOKS

SAN FRANCISCO

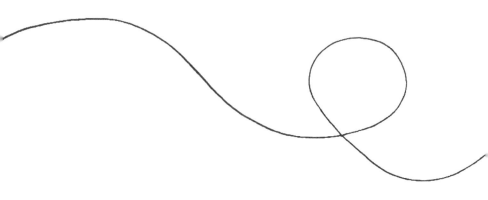

ISBN-13: 978-0-8118-5836-6

Manufactured in Mexico.

Designed by Sarah Meyer
This book was typeset in Dalliance, Fling, and Gotham 8/11.5

Chronicle Books LLC
680 Second Street
San Francisco, California 94107

To my craft muse and mom,

Dely

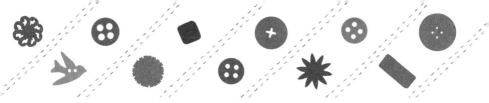

Contents

Introduction

If you have ever muttered the words "I wish I could make a living doing *[insert artistic passion here]*," you certainly are not alone. For a creative individual like yourself, trapped in a dour cubicle transcribing letters for your boss or nursing achy feet after waiting on tables, it's probably a mantra you recite every day. But while your coworkers are eyeing the corner office, your goals lie elsewhere. You ponder throw pillow design possibilities instead of sales reports. Your cubicle contraband provides temporary fodder for your inventiveness—coasters made of paper clips, anybody? With your finger poised over the "quit" button, you yearn for an escape. For now, starting your own creative business may be nothing more than an idea, but it's absolutely possible to turn what you do for fun into what you do to get paid.

These days, it isn't at all surprising to ask a gal where she got the baubles draped around her neck, and find her response paired with a handshake and business card. The urge to make stuff, combined with growing public interest in design and the renewed popularity of traditional art forms like knitting and sewing, has made it more appealing than ever to turn a craft into a business. But how exactly do you make the transition from hobbyist to professional crafter? It might be hard to imagine making this move, especially when you're already holding down a day job to pay the utility bills, school loans, and rent, not to mention spending time with your friends and family. The good news is that with planning and determination you can achieve more than you ever thought possible.

Acting on your desire to earn money from your craft can be an anxiety-filled proposition. Consider *Craft, Inc.* your guide as you prepare for this impending mental and belt-tightening shift. Bridging the gap between your creative vision and the reality of starting a business, this guide provides advice on putting together a business plan, creating a line of goods, outsourcing your production, selling your wares in the wholesale or retail market, and getting editorial coverage in magazines. In addition, to serve as your muses, established indie crafters and designers are interviewed throughout.

The road to making your craft a profitable business can be bumpy. It might take time for your unique style to catch on; even if you become the darling of the indie design scene and gain instant fans, it doesn't necessarily mean you'll turn a profit this year, or next year. Building a successful creative business requires many elements. Some elements are intangible—like luck and timing—and some you can control—like working hard and arming yourself with knowledge. No one can predict or prepare you for every obstacle that will come your way, but in *Craft, Inc.* you'll learn about potential pitfalls and ways to protect your business.

It won't be long until you experience the unbeatable joy of making that first sale, the empowerment of seeing your name on your very own business cards, and the thrill of opening your favorite glossy and spotting your work gracing its pages. Suddenly, you'll find that the creative business dream you've slept on for years will now keep you up at night, giddy with excitement. And while your old career simply put food on the table, your new crafting career will feed your soul. With *Craft, Inc.* on your side, you will be prepared to successfully take this creative leap!

CHAPTER 1

Your Creative Mind

Do you know the extent of your creative potential? It's hard to gauge if you haven't given it any room to grow and develop. Perhaps you're insecure about your talents or indecisive about what crafts to pursue. Or maybe your creative alter ego only appears on special occasions, just in time to create hand-spun woolens for the holidays. How do you respond when thoroughly impressed friends say, "You should sell this!"? Do you allow yourself excuses to avoid going after this dream? Maybe you've abandoned your craft for a more conventional career and you feel there isn't enough room left in your schedule, or perhaps you're afraid of failure. This chapter will help you explore, reclaim, or recharge your creative potential. And because you can't be creative without *creating*, you'll be clued in to the perseverance it takes to turn craft ideas into craft business reality. So gather courage, and your crochet hooks, and get ready to explore the depths of your talents!

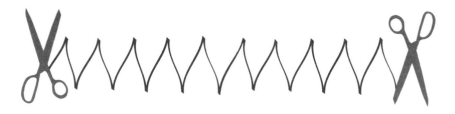

Creative Mythology

For months, or maybe even years, the prospect of becoming a creative-business owner has been sitting patiently inside your head. The part of you that craves stability demands that you stay away from a new career path that you may find intimidating, mysterious, or unpredictable. Since it's not easy to dismiss fears and anxieties completely, why not manage them? Let's start by acknowledging five common myths that many aspiring artists subscribe to; you'll probably recognize yourself in some, if not all, of them.

MYTH **1** **To be an artist you should have a background in fine arts or design.** In this guide, we use the word *artist* in the broadest sense of the term. In essence, an artist is anyone imbued with healthy doses of curiosity and creative urges. You don't need a degree in art or design to qualify as a so-called "real artist." You can be a naturally creative person independent of your educational background. Some of the most successful artists are largely self-taught in their discipline and lack an artistic background or formal training. If this is your situation, it simply means that your creative education will be on an as-needed basis. After all, Tadao Ando, who began practicing architectural design with neither a degree nor training, was awarded the Pritzker Architecture Prize—the world's highest honor in architecture—in 1995.

MYTH **2** **I'm too old to tap into my creativity and start my own creative business.** It's never too late to discover or rediscover your creative talents. Tapping into your creativity is a lifelong process, whether you realize it at age eight or forty-seven. Maybe you'll have to give up being on the "30 Designers Under 30" list, but there are several things you gain with age: more life experiences, greater under-standing of your likes and dislikes, and the ability to clearly articulate your values in your work. In fact, if you are at retirement age, you probably have more free time than most people to pursue a business. Try not to worry about the time that has already passed; just focus on the time ahead. You can create a strong body of work in a relatively short period of time.

MYTH **3** **All of the great ideas have already been done. Someone else can do it better than I ever could.** A classic creative cop-out. With this myth you're basically telling yourself you'll fail before you've even tried. It can be daunting and ambitious to set out to create new trends, but when you remove the pressure to produce something "great" and proceed at your own pace, you'll see that it can be done. Allow yourself to be a beginner. Everyone has creative potential; it just takes time and practice to develop your personal style. Once your creative confidence kicks in, ideas will flow and you'll shake your head wondering why you doubted yourself in the first place.

MYTH **4** **You need to quit your full-time job to make time for your craft.** You don't necessarily need to close one chapter in your career to start a new one. In fact, until you are financially comfortable working full-time on your craft, you should milk every last drop of your steady job. It pays the bills and provides health care and a retirement fund, after all. Squeezing in time on the side for your creative endeavors will require learning how to manage both your time and energy. If your job is so time-consuming that you find yourself working more than forty hours a week or taking work home with you, you may want to consider finding a less demanding job. You can ease out of your wage-paying job as your creative gig begins to grow and demands more of your time. When that time comes, you can negotiate to reduce your work hours or acquire part-time, contract, or freelance jobs until it's time to strike out entirely on your own.

MYTH **5** **You need to wait for the "right time" to start your creative business.** If you're anticipating that the planets will align to create the perfect situation to begin, you might be waiting forever. You may never save quite enough money to finance your new lifestyle and career; you may not have the perfect space to do your craft; and the next big idea may not strike you like lightning. So when is the right time to take your creative ambition off hiatus?

Right now!

LOTTA JANSDOTTER, Brooklyn, New York
Surface Designer, Lifestyle Goods

In 1996, Lotta Anderson began designing home-wares using her striking sense of color and an illustration style inspired by all things natural. The Swedish style maven had just moved to San Francisco and was working for a variety of employers: a restaurant, a printing house, and a textile designer—where she was learning skills that would come in handy later. Though she had no formal training in art or design, her self-professed stubborn, independent personality and a belief in her own creative spirit propelled her to launch a business called Lotta Jansdotter. Although store buyers were skeptical of her penchant for linen fabrics, her fresh, modern-meets-natural aesthetic convinced them to take a chance on her. Over a decade later, with a fan base covering three continents, Lotta Jansdotter's popularity and product offerings both continue to grow, all infused with her hallmark simplicity.

Were you apprehensive about designing your own line without any formal training in art or design?

I don't believe you need a piece of paper, like a diploma, to say you can make art. But, of course, I wasn't really sure that I could make a living being creative. I was very insecure about not knowing how to use a computer. But instead of thinking of it as a limitation, I turned it around and made it my strength. All my illustrations come directly from my sketchbook. There is no manipulation whatsoever using a computer. My work is very organic and simple.

When you first started, what types of products were you selling?

My startup costs were only $500. I had three different cushion styles, each in three different colorways, and a table linen in one design. I was screen-printing everything myself, so I really didn't have the time to produce as many products as I wanted. I did what was comfortable for me. I wanted to control every part of the production process at the time.

At what point did you decide it was time to outsource all of the production?

A couple of years after I had started the business. I was not aggressively looking to outsource production. In fact, I had been resisting it for a while because I knew that managing production and distribution would take away from my creative time. Then I met this Japanese woman (who later licensed my artwork) who had been using a source in Lithuania for her textile work. She set me up with production there.

Was it a very difficult decision to make?

No, I had given it great thought and it was a very natural progression in the business. If I wanted to grow and do trade shows, it would require it. I felt I had gone as far as I could all on my own engine. Plus, I didn't want to live without at least trying it out. I wouldn't want to spend my time wondering "what if."

Speaking of Japan, you have a large fan base there! How did that happen?

Well, back in 1997, I met that Japanese buyer of home goods (the same one who set me up with production in Lithuania) through a friend I'd met while I was checking out a trade show. I had given her a business card I had made, which at the time I had screen-printed onto some remnant card stock. She asked me if I would be willing to license my artwork so she could use it to make postcards and sell them at shows and retail stores in Japan. I agreed, and they did so well that she asked me for six more designs. It just snowballed and more and more people became interested. I later decided to invest in a plane ticket to Japan. I figured, what could it hurt? So I went to Japan and did an exhibition there. Luckily, this woman shared with me her editorial contacts in Japan, including Zakka, a boutique retailer and publisher. Zakka was very instrumental in promoting my work, publishing whole magazines about me. Taking that risk and going to Japan was the best investment I had ever made. »

Very serendipitous meeting that woman! Now, as a popular designer, you've seen your work emulated by other independent designers and even large companies. How do you deal with that?

In the beginning, I was really paranoid about it because it's really difficult to stop people from copying your style. I don't get too upset anymore because I feel it's unproductive. Early on in the business, it can be a little threatening, but as you grow, you let go of those insecurities. People who copy really haven't developed as artists. They have no integrity or ethics in their work. I have had to use an intellectual property lawyer to go after artists who were directly infringing on my copyright—like using my exact illustrations in their paintings! As for the larger companies, they really should just contact me and ask me to license my work instead of making a knockoff version.

What role does being a designer play in your life?

It's one and the same. My business and my lifestyle can't be separated. The business is me.

What's next for you?

I have so many ideas! If only I had the time to complete all of them. Right now, my mind is really on the longevity of my brand. As a creative-business owner, you have to keep renewing yourself. It's all part of progressing and moving forward.

What's Your Creative Bug?

If you've been enmeshed in your craft for ages, go ahead and skip this section. But if you don't have the faintest idea of your creative purpose, just a vague yearning to create, you'll have to find the art form that's best for you. It's important to start with an endeavor that comes naturally to you. It may be helpful to look to your previous creative habits as a child or teenager. Perhaps you'll rediscover how much you enjoy an activity that was "2 cool + 2 be = 4 gotten"—like making dioramas or friendship bracelets!

Whatever craft you decide to pursue, it should be something you love to do regularly, maybe even every day. Sure, enameling sounds like fun. But can you imagine doing it all the time? Would you do it even if you weren't paid to do it? Don't choose a craft because you hear it's a real moneymaker or you've got a natural talent. You should love what you're doing: when you do, you will be dedicated enough to do it well. When you don't, you'll struggle with procrastination and your results may not be as satisfying; and it will be more difficult to get through the lean times and the busy times.

Zeroing in on your place in the creative universe can be as spontaneous as love at first sight, or it can be a trial and error process. However you go about your search, it's best not to employ a shotgun approach. Instead, begin with a single endeavor that you find satisfying or fascinating. A class at your local craft store or community college is a great way to start. Learning about a particular craft is almost like getting to know a person. Sometimes your initial impression may not be favorable, but when you make the effort to really know your craft and study its every nuance, you'll learn to appreciate, understand, and maybe even love it. With time, you may even declare yourself an expert. After you've exploited as much as you can from one craft, maybe you've created scented candles for every room in your home, then it might be time to try your hand at a different one.

Understandably, choosing one craft at a time may be difficult. Once your creative moxie kicks in, suddenly every art form becomes a fertile area of exploration. Creative folks tend to run themselves ragged dipping their hands into every pot and acting on every whim the instant it pops into their heads. Their enthusiasm for starting new projects usually far outstrips their time or budget to do them. If you juggle too many competing projects, you'll likely feel fatigued, overwhelmed, and maybe even resentful when projects don't manifest as expected. It might not be easy, but it's important to pace yourself.

Continuously making projects will help reveal what you love to do. Through it all, certain processes, methods, and artistic creations will ring true to you. Maybe you'll love crafts that require painstaking attention to detail. Or perhaps you'll find that you yearn to work with natural materials. Ultimately, you'll learn which crafts you like or don't like, thereby adding and subtracting from your repertoire of talents.

Building Creative Confidence

Being a creative person is a matter of how you perceive yourself. If you think you are creative, then you are! If you don't think you are, then you never will be. It's all about having confidence—the single most important quality to have in a creative business. And confidence does not mean arrogance; it means taking an optimistic approach. By practicing your craft regularly and maintaining a "can-do" attitude and a strong belief in your creative worth, you'll find your confidence growing. So start building that experience by making things now!

Let's say you have a passion for fiber arts and a beginner's capacity to knit, but you don't know exactly what you want to make. What should you do? Start somewhere, start small, and start simple. That probably means making a hat rather than a floor-length knit coat with a contrasting collar and handmade buttons. The first step is often the hardest to take. If you worry that you don't know enough of a craft, acquire skills as you need them. There is no right way to begin nor is there a foolproof step-by-step approach to developing your creativity. Just hit the pavement running and forget the big picture—you might surprise yourself.

Your initial projects may run the spectrum from hideous eyesore to visually stunning. If you believe that a true artist churns out perfection every time, you're sadly mistaken. Many designers don't know their product in exact detail at the beginning. They sketch, compose several prototypes, and probably make numerous mistakes before arriving at the finished product. Even the most accomplished artist will produce mediocre work during his development. So don't worry too much about results now; this is not the time to be your harshest critic. Consider this your creative laboratory phase—your initial projects are seeds for further development. The point is to begin unlocking your creativity. Remember to give yourself props for achieving any goal, however small, especially when attempting something you never thought you could do. Be your own head cheerleader.

Once you start channeling your inner artist on a regular basis, you never know what she's going to make you do: enroll in a leather-tooling class, emblazon a skull on a tea cozy, or restore an antique ceramic mermaid to its full kitsch glory. When your creative sensibilities are at the helm, you'll find yourself looking at something—be it a pair of chandelier earrings or a bar of fragrant soap—and thinking, "I could've made that!" Now that's creative confidence.

Craft Time

When a big chunk of your day goes toward making a living, you may not have the initiative, much less the energy, to work on your creative pursuits. Sometimes all you really want to do is veg in front of the tube or imbibe into the wee hours with pals. To support your blossoming creative career, you'll have to readjust your schedule and your thinking so that your craft gets top billing on your priority list; finding time is not impossible, but you'll have to be extra disciplined and responsible. Try keeping a time journal for a week, being honest about where your time goes. You might find those few extra hours in unexpected places, like maybe skimming half an hour off your lunch break so that you can leave work early, or perhaps cooking a week's worth of dinners at once to buy a whole afternoon to yourself. However, sleep and regular meals are not expendable items. Be careful not to surrender all of your downtime; you'll still need time to relax.

You will need to make a conscious effort to make your craft a part of your life. Start by committing a specific number of hours to the craft grindstone. Think in bite-size portions at first, like two or three hours a week, preferably at times that are reliably quiet. Listen to your natural body rhythms and select a window of time when your energy is at its highest. It may mean taking a rain check on an invitation to sip chai lattes or recording your favorite TV shows for later viewing. If you're a parent, you might have to take your kids to the babysitter or ask your spouse to watch them without interruption. The trick is to develop a ritual that will evolve into a habit. You'll enjoy diving into your craft so much that you'll find yourself steadily adding hours to your craft regimen without much thought.

You should always begin your creative two-hour window with goals; without any, you'll likely succumb to the "P" word, as in *procrastinate,* and find yourself catching up on correspondence, sorting laundry, or surfing eBay—anything to avoid the hard bits of your artwork. If you have trouble staying focused during your craft hours, try scheduling smaller slots of time for yourself, taking craft classes to develop your skills, or interning for a local indie designer.

GIVE YOURSELF A JUMP START

If two or three craft hours a week is too slow for you, consider taking a sabbatical from work (otherwise known as using up some of your vacation hours) to give yourself time for a craft intensive. To exploit these "empty" days to their fullest potential, you will need to fill them with energy, tasks, and deadlines. Try taking one day off at a time, at first, or schedule a month of Fridays off. Otherwise, the vast potential of each day may overwhelm you, allowing creative paralysis to kick in.

A Room with a Muse

You'll probably both practice your craft and start your creative business within your home. Bear in mind that when your home and business share a space, it gives a whole new meaning to the word housework—you'll make a mess and have even less time to clean it up. Working from home, you'll also be subjected to a variety of disruptions, such as personal phone calls, unexpected visitors, dog walks, and unplanned family dilemmas. So it remains absolutely imperative to be disciplined and stick to a schedule: get plenty of sleep, take breaks, and minimize distractions like television or chatting online.

Decorate your space so that you're excited and energized to be there.

It's also important to get your home organized before making it the venue for your cottage industry. Start by designating a place that allows you to work without constant interruption. This creative cocoon can be a desk, closet, wall, spare room, garage, basement, or even a corner. (An armoire with a pullout desk inside is an elegant way to hide your supplies in plain sight.) Decorate your space so that you're excited and energized to be there. There will be days that you'll have to drag yourself through your crafting—especially as orders pile up. It is on these days that keeping an inspired work space becomes most important. And remember: even if your space is small, that doesn't mean that big ideas or big projects can't emerge from it.

Tips to keep your space inspired:

Make your space a reflection of yourself, whether that means being colorful or minimalist.

Maintain an inspiration board or wire and hang photographs, clippings, and swatches. Feel free to layer images over one another and to change images often to follow your whims and interests.

Surround yourself with things you find beautiful. If something bothers you, consider moving it to another area, out of sight.

Have ample task lighting. Especially if you like working in dark, intimate spaces, enough task lighting will prevent you from straining your eyes.

Take advantage of natural light, as it can often stimulate your energy.

Play music that energizes your creative spirit.

Have invigorating refreshments handy, like a cup of herbal tea.

Keep your space stocked with essentials, like pens, paper, yarn, or embroidery floss. You don't want to spend time looking for these items when you should be working.

If you like your space neat when you work, make sure it is clean before your designated craft hours begin. When your craft time is limited, you don't want to spend it tidying up.

You need a table that accommodates your work. Use an actual table—the floor or bed does not count—with an ergonomic chair. For times when a worktable is not necessary, find a comfortable place to work, but not one so comfortable that you're lulled into drowsy ineffectiveness.

Organize your work space for efficiency and you'll be more productive. Invest in storage shelves and organizers. Even if you're the type that loves to be disorganized, your paperwork never should be.

JILL BLISS, Santa Rosa, California
Eco-Conscious Crafts

What do you get when you pair a background in farming with a degree in design? Illustrations and creations inspired by nature that exude an authenticity some designers spend a lifetime trying to cultivate. Jill Bliss's reputation for putting reinvention at a premium is well deserved. For her, green design is not just a catchphrase but a lifestyle commitment: she uses recycled paper and soy-based inks, and even co-opted her boyfriend's childhood bedsheets as fodder for her creations. Jill's craft business began accidentally when she found herself jobless, like many other Web designers, after the dot-com bubble burst in 2001. With her free time, she began creating unique items like paper earrings and plush birds. Five years later, her work still carries the same spontaneity and honesty, earning her legions of loyal fans.

How did you get started selling?

After undergrad at Parsons, I moved back to San Francisco, where I met a lot of other creative people who were also making goods. That's when Blissen came to be, a collective-cum-consignment shop, where the participants would sell their work. It became so complicated juggling everyone's schedules that it crashed and burned, and most of the members have moved on to other things. I use the Blissen Web site now to sell my production line projects. (I also maintain another Web site for my freelance portfolio of illustration and design work.) In the beginning, I also would sell my work in person. My boyfriend has a record label for indie pop bands and, during shows, I would hawk my goods on the merchandise table. I started making one-off goods with found materials and they would sell out. So I started making items in larger editions, like ten, and then those would sell out, so I began making even more.

Was it difficult to produce more?

Luckily, my previous jobs have served me well. My background in fashion came in handy. I worked for five years in the fashion industry. I worked for several small fashion companies as a production manager, where I learned everything inside out—especially how to craft something more efficiently. I keep my home studio very organized. People are very surprised to see how minimalist it really is. It also helped that my parents used to own a farm; that really instilled a self-starter work ethic within me. In farming I learned to be very resourceful. We would also make crafts like quilts and spice ropes on the farm during the holidays.

You always seem to have new stuff on your Web site. How often do you generate new work?

I like to make new things, whether for myself or for my business, every two to three weeks. For the business, I generally like to put new items on the Web site every three to four weeks to keep it fresh. It sometimes makes me a little frantic, but I thrive on that energy.

Do you ever worry about anyone knocking off your work?

Not really. The larger illustrations take about 30 hours or more to complete, and the designs are constantly evolving from my past projects. If someone wants to copy my work or work process, there's no getting around the amount of effort and care each piece requires. Once someone's spent that kind of time and care on something, it will have become their own, hopefully. Plus, all my work is copyrighted.

Is there an accomplishment you're most proud of?

I feel especially proud when someone takes the time to e-mail me or approach me at an event to tell me how much my work has helped them with their own life or work! I've always done the same thing with people whose work I admire. It's important to let them know their value—and it's just so amazing to me that I'm now becoming one of those people myself! For instance, it's very exciting to hear from other creators who've adopted recycled materials in their own work because they've seen what I've done with recycled materials. To have that kind of influence on someone you've never met is almost indescribable. It's a huge responsibility, but very rewarding, and a much greater feeling of pride than getting a magazine article or store placement.

THE MORE THE MERRIER

They go by different names: crafting mafias or ubiquitous Stitch 'n' Bitch groups. No matter the label, they're a group of people coming together in the name of craft, mutual support, and general merriment. When you're going it alone with your craft, you can feel isolated, heightening your need to connect with other individuals. The benefits of being part of a larger entity are numerous: The group can be a support system to help you complete partially finished projects and curb any crafting ADD, and it can act as a vehicle to attract attention to your work. You might even raise your craft cred by associating with the more prominent members of such a group. Organizers are usually selective when choosing new members, gauging new entrants' seriousness and ability to actively participate. If you are thinking about starting a group of your own, understand that collectives work best when participants meet regularly and live in the same general area. Without a regimented meeting schedule, the excitement and momentum of the collective can be lost. Once it's gone, it can be hard to recapture. Keep the energy going by planning a whole year's worth of events and staying connected through an online forum for discussion, announcements, and feedback.

Sharing Your Dream

In the beginning, you may be secretive about your dream to start a creative business. It takes fortitude to announce what may seem lofty or foolish to others. But there is power in making your dream known. You

> As you present your ideas both verbally and visually, you'll start to understand your work better.

may be motivated by other people's expectations. A friend might connect you with another aspiring crafter or even a patron for your homemade quilts. And, importantly, as you present your ideas both verbally and visually, you'll start to understand your work better.

At the same time, you will need to be careful about who you choose to share your dreams with. For instance, your nearest and dearest friends and family members, especially those who are more occupationally sensible or traditional, may not be able to wrap their heads around the idea of quitting a well-paying job for a potentially unstable business that depends on your creative abilities. Long-standing assumptions die hard, so if your dream may not make your mother proud, share it with her later, when you've got finished products or sales receipts to show. Avoid the naysayers, those people who don't understand what you're doing and

Trust your own instincts; the path you choose and the fruits of your labor will be unique and the outcome could be even better than you imagine.

therefore impose their fears upon you. (Like you didn't have enough apprehensions already!) Conversely, you don't want blind support and 100% positive reinforcement all the time, either.

If your creative pronouncements are falling on deaf ears, a good way to circumvent negative or indifferent reactions is to surround yourself with a network of like-minded folks (see "The More the Merrier," facing page). Connecting with other creative individuals in the trenches is a good way to spin your creative compass and refuel your motivation. It's probably best to find a kindred spirit in similar shoes, one with a parallel groove, so that you can pursue your goals in unison or perhaps work on collaborative projects. If you don't have friends handy who fit these criteria, you can find other individuals disposed toward craft through blogs, online craft communities, or local craft classes.

You should be aware that the bohemian community can be equal parts nurturing and competitive. Some artists are very altruistic, offering free advice and guidance. On the other hand, don't feel too bad if any of your dream buddies or mentors reject your advances for friendship. Some artists are extremely busy, and cautious too. You can't really blame a crafter for protecting her intellectual property, material sources, manufacturers, or trade secrets; she worked hard to acquire them.

If you can't befriend your craft muses, you can learn about them through interviews (like the ones in this guide) or through their Web sites or blogs. And although it is helpful to use their success stories as models, following the same paths may not guarantee similar results for you. Trust your own instincts; the path you choose and the fruits of your labor will be unique, and the outcome could be even better than you imagine.

CHAPTER 2

Your Business Mind

Now that your creative mind is primed for action, it's time to switch gears and mold your business acumen. Beginning right now, you should start treating your craft business as a real business, not just a hobby. Your frame of mind shouldn't be limited to earning a little supplemental income or creating a business just for fun. Be serious and be professional, because you never know where this might lead. To help with the adjustment, Chapter 2 will introduce you to terms like *sole proprietor, fictitious business name,* and *limited liability company.* But before you fill out any forms or pull out the plastic, you'll need to ask yourself how ready you are for entrepreneurship. In a world where we can get daily assistance from day-care providers, personal trainers, and dog walkers, being a business owner means doing the exact opposite: being completely self-reliant, working ridiculous hours, and wearing several different hats simultaneously—a veritable jack- or jill-of-all-trades. Are you ready?

QUIZ: Are You Entrepreneur Material?

Most people believe they have what it takes (or that it doesn't take much) to be a business owner. And although anyone can *start* a business, it takes a certain breed to make it a long-lasting, profitable venture. Taking this quiz will assess your aptitude for entrepreneurship.

1 **If you were going snowboarding for the first time, you would most likely . . .**

A. Sign up for a snowboarding class before joining your friends on the slopes.

B. Change your mind at the last minute and toboggan alone instead.

C. Throw caution to the wind and take the lift straight up to the double black-diamond slope.

2 **How would you describe your sock drawer?**

A. I try to pair my socks when I can, but I usually have to hunt for the matching pair.

B. My socks are all paired and then organized by color.

C. Does my hamper count as a sock drawer?

3 **As a member of a wedding entourage, you've been asked to participate in a favor-making party that starts at noon and ends at three o'clock. At the gathering, you would typically be the person that . . .**

A. Plays video games or reads magazines until the bride notices that you haven't been assigned a task. You also leave at three o'clock on the dot.

B. Volunteers for any task. You also take it upon yourself to re-tie every bow that looks sloppy and re-cut any tag lacking perfect right angles.

C. Is picky about your task assignment. You hate getting your fingers sticky with glue.

4 You befriend another crafter who seems like a sweet and talented individual, but your inner voice tells you that this person is going to be trouble. You would . . .

A. Trust your instincts above all else; you would never return this person's e-mails.

B. Ask other crafters for their opinions of this person.

C. Consider the advantages (her friend is an editor at *Lucky*) and disadvantages (she's clingy) of befriending this crafter.

5 Your embroidered handkerchiefs have been on the market for nearly a year. You've tried two different types of packaging and even tested them at different price points, but sales continue to plummet. Your first instinct would be to . . .

A. Go to the library and pick up a book on improving sales.

B. Ask friends and colleagues for their opinions or suggestions.

C. Give up on the handkerchiefs and try your hand at greeting cards instead.

6 You ask a friend to help man your booth at the New York International Gift Fair. When she arrives, you notice her G-string rising above her jeans like a slingshot. You would most likely . . .

A. Ask her to go home and put on more professional attire.

B. Fire her on the spot.

C. Pretend not to notice and hope that buyers and members of the media will not be offended.

7 Which statement best describes your attitude when you get into an argument:

A. I'm always right.

B. I can admit when I'm wrong and I have no problem apologizing.

C. I would rather be quiet than admit I'm wrong.

8 You and another jewelry designer started your businesses in unison. However, her jewelry is more popular, garnering more sales and press mentions. Your plan would be to . . .

A. Start working on your press kit to mail to magazine editors.

B. Do nothing and figure she's just lucky.

C. Copy her metalworking technique—this is business, after all.

9 Working as a graphic designer, you've made several wedding invitations. You've gotten praise for your work and know you'd make money if you made a business out of it. But you're not very enthusiastic about dealing with brides. You would . . .

A. Go ahead and do it even though you'd probably hate it. Hey, it'll make you money!

B. Psych yourself into believing that working with brides isn't that difficult.

C. Walk away from the idea and think of better business ideas.

ANSWERS:

1. (A) *Sign me up for a class on the bunny slope, please.* Although successful entrepreneurs have an appetite for adventure, they wouldn't make a reckless decision. They prefer to minimize risk by arming themselves with the proper knowledge and skills to increase their rate of success.

2. (B) *My sock drawer would make Martha proud.* The most efficient business owners are organized. They manage their time, juggling tax, shipping, press, and trade show deadlines, and they keep receipts and paperwork in a filing system. Even if they are cluttered by nature, they know better than to extend disorganization into their businesses.

3. (B) *I always strive to be the best worker of the bunch.* The best entre-preneurs have good work habits. They are often meticulous, devoting themselves to the task at hand. Self-motivated to boot, they don't need someone to tell them what to do. They have no problem looking to themselves for leadership and support. They also aren't afraid to do any of the less-than-glamorous tasks, like mopping spilled ink off the floor or unloading cumbersome boxes off a freight truck. They are more than willing to put in the elbow grease, effort, and extra hours to complete a job, even if it means working longer than anticipated.

4. (C) *Instinct isn't everything.* Possessing a sharp instinct is a valuable asset, but good business owners know better than to rely on that alone. They try to assess a situation from all angles and use all the tools available to them before reaching a final decision.

5. (B) *I'm not afraid to ask my friends and colleagues for help.* Although creative-business owners are natural do-it-yourself types, smart entrepreneurs know when it's time to seek wisdom from others. They eagerly learn lessons from their failures and aren't afraid to make known their shortcomings when they need help.

6. (A) *My company comes first.* Attentive entrepreneurs make choices that are in the best interest of the company. They would not ignore problems that are hurting the business. They also thrive in challenging situations. When circumstances are particularly awkward, they look for alternate solutions.

7. (B) *I can't always be right.* Intelligent business owners know that most problems are not usually black or white. Regardless of the situation, they are diplomatic at all times and do their best to please clients. They are able to make sacrifices, even if it means setting aside their ego, to succeed.

8. (A) *I can make my own luck.* All business owners are competitive, but conscientious ones do so without losing their integrity. Although it's normal to be jealous of someone else's success, they realize it's better to turn that energy into action instead. Smart entrepreneurs know that success is not mostly luck. Through hard work and determination, they know they can influence their destiny.

9. (C) *For my business, I'd rather do what I love.* Even though the goal of any business is ultimately to make money, most successful business owners truly love what they do. They would engage in their craft even if they weren't paid to do it.

HOW DID YOU DO?

For each correct answer, give yourself a point. If you scored five points or more correctly, congratulations! Your instincts are pointing you toward entrepreneurship. If you scored four or less, don't despair. Not everyone who runs their own business was born with an entrepreneurial chip in their brain. Luckily, anyone with passion, commitment, and perseverance can learn to become a good entrepreneur.

Business Plan Basics

A goal as big as starting your own creative business needs definite plans. How many items will you have in your debut collection? How often will you introduce a new line of goods? Who's your target market? What's your marketing plan? What if your business fails? All of these issues should be addressed at the beginning. Most people are intimidated by business plans, or what may seem like the daunting task of creating one. Just think of them as a map for your business; if you don't know where you're going, you might find it difficult to get there.

Unless you're looking for outside funding (like from a banking institution), your business plan will largely be for your own eyes, so make it as formal or informal as you like. It can be businesslike—neatly drafted on a word processing program and bound in a presentation folder—or craftlike—handwritten in a journal and decorated with collage and illustrations. It can even be as simple as putting together a list of measurable goals and objectives for the business. Below are topics to consider including in your business plan:

❧ Projected Timeline

❧ Company Description

❧ Location and Place of Business

❧ List of Owners and Responsibilities

❧ Creative Mission Statement

❧ Company Identity

❧ Target Market

❧ Market Research

❧ Products Offered and Frequency of Release

❧ Projected Goods in Debut Line

❧ Equipment and Materials

❧ Production

❧ Selling Strategies

❧ Marketing Plan

❧ Financial Plan (including budget for first year)

❧ Revenue Projections

❧ Exit Plan

Don't worry if there are terms here that you don't recognize. You will learn most of them as you read further, and the "Internet Resources" section on page 156 will point you in the right direction to learn the rest. It is best to start with a plan in place, however rough, knowing it will change over time. This plan will create a foundation for your business, so it is important that you dedicate a good deal of time and thought to it. Using the aforementioned topics, create your business plan step-by-step, first filling in the pieces you understand, then clarifying and adding information as it all begins to make more sense.

Designing Your New Career

Earning a living off your creativity is not just about making things that people will want to buy. It's also about making your livelihood, well . . . *lively!* You have the opportunity to reinvent your career on your own terms and mold your business into an ideal work environment. As you are basically designing your new lifestyle, you should incorporate elements that you find stimulating. For example, if you love to travel and snap photographs, maybe you should launch a line of travel journals using screen-printed versions of your snapshots. If you're a community-minded individual, you might also think about ways that your company can help support charitable organizations. Perhaps you'll design a brooch,

Earning a living off your creativity is not just about making things that people will want to buy. It's also about making your livelihood, well . . . *lively!*

modeled after your grandmother's heirloom piece, whose proceeds support cancer research, or maybe you'll increase your profit margin enough to allow you to donate a quarter of your profits to a women's shelter. Take advantage of this embryonic stage of your business and synthesize activities you love or organizations you'd like to support into your new creative career.

SUNSHINE'S SCARVES, Los Angeles, California
Crocheted Scarves

For some individuals, crafting is a therapeutic, stress-relieving technique—as was the case for Joy Durham, a single mother of two, who found herself clutching crochet hooks as she watched her five-year-old daughter, Sunshine, endure 12 eye surgeries after an accident. Fueled by the desire to give her children proper Christmas presents under belt-tightening circumstances, she generated a unique crochet style as she made scarves for them. Her daughter loved hers so much that she refused to take it off. From that moment, Joy's life purpose began to reveal itself. Soon thereafter, she launched a business—making scarves, with plans to donate a portion of the profit to a foundation for prosthetic eye care. Naturally, the business and foundation could only be named after Sunshine. Born of a tragic event, the business is very personal, with a word-of-mouth marketing strategy that relies primarily on the energy radiating from the business and the inspiring story behind it.

How did you come up with the idea to create a company that donates a portion of its profit to a foundation?

I had been selling the scarves strictly by word of mouth, and another dimension began to come together when I was at Sunshine's doctor's office. I noticed that there was a low-income family being turned away for prosthetic care for an eye injury. I asked her doctor, "How can you turn them away?" since I knew the injuries would end up as deformities. That's when I learned that most insurance plans don't cover this type of procedure and that there was no foundation for prosthetic eye care. It became apparent that I should bring the two ideas together: having a company (the scarves) and donating a portion of its profit to a new foundation (prosthetic eye care). That's how the Sunshine Foundation came to be. It became clear to me that this is the reason behind everything we've gone through.

Do you run your business and foundation full-time?

I've been doing commercials and modeling work for 16 years, and I continue to support my family that way. I somehow manage to juggle that with the business and foundation. What makes it a little easier is that my business's product, the scarf, is seasonal. The demand for it starts in August and ends around February, which leaves the other months to cultivate my other career and work on the foundation.

Two young children, a business, a foundation, and a career in front of the camera—you sound tremendously busy! Are you also making all the scarves?

In the very beginning, I was making all the scarves, anywhere from 20 to 50 scarves a month. I decided to stick with scarves only because it's one of the easiest and simplest knitting projects to make. I do have other people helping me make the scarves now, but it's still a bit difficult to teach someone else how to crochet the way I do. I learned to crochet as a child and developed a technique that is apparently difficult to copy. (So I don't worry about people copying my work because it comes with its own protection, so to speak.) I've had avid crocheters sit and watch me— and they can't even comprehend what I'm doing. It all comes naturally to me. I don't even know if the stitches are proper, so it would be difficult to write out a pattern.

Did working in the film and television industry help you get your scarves into the media and celebrities' hands?

I think it's helped me, but truly it's all happened quite serendipitously. For example, someone who worked at CNN got one of my scarves and fell in love with the story behind it. They contacted me and asked if they could do an interview. Sunshine's Scarves became one of seven top picks for Christmas 2003 on CNN. It really catapulted the business forward. I got an onslaught of orders that kept me busy until March of the following year.

And when I do commercial work, I often sit on the set for five to six hours, but only work like an hour and half of it, so I always bring my yarns and crochet while I wait. Sometimes I'll find a crowd of people around me asking what I'm doing—and I might end up selling 15 to 20 scarves that day! Some of the stylists who buy them will sometimes use them for future jobs. One stylist dressed up Sela Ward for a magazine cover. Another stylist worked on the set of *Friends.* On one of the last episodes, Jennifer »

Aniston's character received a Sunshine scarf for Christmas. Jennifer went on to purchase some scarves for herself.

Thankfully, it's all happened so effortlessly, as though the company was generating its own PR. I almost feel like I should have done more work to get to this point. I just hope that people continue to act on inspiration. It's such a beautiful thing when people ask me, "How can I help?" or say, "This is an amazing company and cause." And best of all, it's not a cheap product. There are a lot of people who get the scarf to support my cause and are delightfully surprised when they find such a high-quality product that uses exquisite European yarns.

What do you hope people will glean from the story of your business?

When you're planning a business, it doesn't have to be a self-centered scenario. The business doesn't have to be about making money; it can be about giving to your community. Having a charitable component is an incredible way to get people involved in your business. They'll see a company outside of its profit margin, and for business owners, customers will be more than just a paycheck.

Naming Your Baby

Naming your business is an important decision—right up there with naming your firstborn child. You should start by making a list of names and surveying your friends, family, and colleagues for their opinions or suggestions. Go eponymous (like Angela Adams). Go clever (like Good on Paper Design). Or go humorous (like Cookie and the Dude). Whatever you choose, it should match your company's goods and aesthetic. Like you would for your own child's name, say the business name aloud to make sure it rolls off the tongue nicely. Ask yourself if the business name will still sound good to you ten years from now, when you're older and more mature, and if the name allows you the flexibility to grow and expand. For example, "Edge Bedding" would be a confusing name if, at a later point, you decide you'd like to design tote bags, too.

As fun as it may be to come up with a nifty name, a business name is not something to take lightly. You will need to do your homework, part of which will include doing a national search for other companies using the same name. One way to search is to check for Internet domain names that use your prospective company name. (You'll probably want a Web site sooner or later, so keep this in mind if the domain name you want is available—you might want to take steps to reserve it.) You'll also want to check with state and federal agencies to see if another company has trademarked the name you've chosen, or you run the risk of hearing from a lawyer with a cease-and-desist order. This is true even if you decide to use your own name. Once you've paid licenses and permits, stamped your company name onto checks and business cards, and launched a Web site, it could be a costly and major pain if you are forced to change everything.

Business Essentials

Whether you plan to hawk goods on the side or in bulk to retail stores, the instant you sell your work for a profit, you're technically in business and, therefore, subject to taxes, rules, laws, and regulations. You will have to apply for a variety of licenses and permits, and you'll need to consider protective measures like health insurance and product liability insurance. Here are the basic necessities for starting your own business:

Business License
To legally run a business, you have to apply for a business license in your city. There is usually a nominal fee to pay, and, when you renew your license yearly, there will be a renewal fee (sometimes called business tax), the amount usually dependent on your business's total revenue. You are often required to keep this license mounted on a wall at your place of business.

Zoning
In conjunction with getting a business license, city officials will verify that you are able to run your type of business at your location. In most cases, cities will allow you to operate your craft business out of your home, as long as you don't post advertisements and your craft isn't something that could potentially rile up the neighbors, like noisy metalwork. If zoning for your location doesn't allow for your specific craft, you may need to apply for a special use permit.

Fictitious Business Name
If you are running your business under a name other than your legal or personal name, you will need to file a Fictitious Business Name, referred to as a "DBA" (Doing Business As), through your county clerk. You will also be required to run an advertisement in a local paper announcing your DBA, and supply a copy of this ad to the county clerk. For many

small newspapers, running these ads is a form of regular revenue. After you apply, you'll often get a solicitation from one of the papers offering to run your ad. Many of them will even send the ad to the county clerk on your behalf.

Certificate of Resale

If you are selling taxable goods, you will need to apply for a certificate of resale, or seller's permit, through the state agency responsible for collecting sales tax (e.g., in California, it's the State Board of Equalization). Unless your state does not have any sales tax, you must collect sales tax on every retail sale made within your state. You will be required to file sales tax returns on a monthly, quarterly, or yearly basis (depending on your sales volume). In these returns, you must provide your total receipts and how much tax you collected within a certain time period. Sales delivered to goods outside your state and wholesale sales are both exempt from sales tax. Whenever anyone purchases items from you at wholesale cost, they need to provide you with an active seller's permit. Likewise, when you want to increase your profitability and buy materials at wholesale cost without paying sales tax, you will have to present your resale number.

Federal Tax ID

If you are a sole proprietor without any employees, you do not need to obtain a Federal Tax ID number, often called an Employer ID Number (EIN). Your individual Social Security number is sufficient for filing taxes. If your company is a partnership or a corporation, or if you have employees, you will need to obtain a Federal Tax ID number through the IRS.

Trademarks

A trademark is a word or phrase (like your business name, slogan, or product name), symbol or picture (like your logo), or any combination of these things that distinguishes your goods from another company's. Getting a trademark is a protective measure to prevent someone else from opening a company or selling a product with the same name. You've probably doodled a million possible trademarks for your business, but those names and logos aren't yours until you make an official trademark request to the government. To file a trademark, you must first do a trade-mark search, either on your own, through a search firm, or with the help of an attorney. If the trademark is available, you can register it on both state (through the state agency that does business filings) and federal (through the U.S. Patent and Trademark Office) levels. The application process can take anywhere from a few months to over a year and, once completed, will grant you ownership of the trademark for ten years.

Home Insurance

If you are running a home-based business, you should talk to your insurance agent to cover any tools, equipment, materials, and inventory you have stored in your home. There may be optional riders you can add to your policy in case a fire should break out in a space dedicated to your business, like your garage. And if customers will be coming into your space, you may want to consider increasing the personal liability insurance on your policy.

Health Insurance

Although it can take a bite out of your wallet, health insurance is something you cannot afford to be without. These days, there are numerous health coverage plans that serve a variety of budgets and needs. You can even join an artists' guild or association to take advantage of health insurance group rates. If you are married or have a domestic partner, you may be able to add yourself to your partner's employee-sponsored health care coverage. If you are quitting your full-time job to launch your own business, take advantage of the opportunity to extend your health insurance through COBRA (Consolidated Omnibus Budget Reconciliation Act). COBRA allows for you, your spouse, and your dependents to maintain continued health insurance for a limited time. When you're running your own business, you'll probably be subjecting yourself to tasks that are physically and mentally taxing, usually at a high-efficiency pace. And when a business runs solely on your fuel, your health and well-being are integral to the success of that business, which, in turn, makes having proper health insurance all the more important.

Product Liability Insurance

Product liability insurance covers you if someone suffers an injury from your product and decides to sue you. In general, most craft or gift products are relatively harmless and don't require that you get this type of insurance. The most "dangerous" crafts are in the candle-making or bath and body fields: a poorly made candle could cause a fire, and creams and soaps could contain potential skin irritants. But even in these fields, the occurrence of a lawsuit may be relatively low. The cost of liability insurance will be dependent on the type of product you produce and how wide the distribution is. You can also get general liability insurance to cover your products.

Phone Line

Legally, you can't print your home number as your business number, so you'll need a business line. These days, people often use their cell phone as their business line. But it might be better to have a dedicated phone line so that you'll always know how to answer phone calls—especially important when buyers or members of the media are contacting you.

Business Bank Account

Before you spend another dime on your business, you should get a separate bank account. It is illegal to use personal bank accounts for business purposes, since they do not clearly separate personal purchases from those that are business-related. To open an account for a business using a DBA, you will need to show proof that you've filed a Fictitious Business Name statement with the county clerk. You will want to choose a banking institution that is nearby if you'll need to deposit checks often. The ideal business checking account would offer flexibility in the allowable number of checks written per month, a reduced minimum balance requirement, and a minimal monthly fee. If you have a business partner, you can require that both partners sign each check so that no single partner can write a check without the other person's knowledge. Also consider opening a savings account to set aside money collected as sales tax—this should help reduce the temptation to spend it and then find yourself short when tax-filing time rolls around.

IRS Publications

As a business, you will be responsible for taxes on all levels: federal, state, county, and city. To differentiate businesses from hobbyists, entities are considered businesses if they are truly making an attempt to generate a profit. A company must be profitable in three out of five years of operation or it may be considered a hobby, in which case you will only be able to deduct expenses up to the total income. You should read IRS publications or speak to a certified public accountant to find out which types of expenses are deductible and how to file your taxes.

A Team or Solo Effort

When you're jumping into the mysterious waters of business ownership, you may think it would be a good idea to have a partner to dive in with you. Since running a business requires so much work, it seems logical that the workload would be lighter when shared by two or three. But this is not true for all partnerships—sometimes things move even slower since decisions have to be approved by the group. Simple mathematics dictate that more people means increased start-up capital for the business; it also means sharing the returns. But partnerships are not simply about dividing labor and profits. In many ways, it's like marriage—behavior and expectations play a large role in the happiness of those in the union. And, like spouses, you and your partner will be spending a tremendous amount of time together. Partnerships can be satisfying when operating like a well-oiled machine and emotionally draining when things aren't running as smoothly.

The best partnerships are those that take advantage of each individual's strengths. And it's even better when each partner brings a different skill to the table—maybe one partner is a graphic design whiz who can build and manage the Web site, while another partner has a background in public relations. Good partnerships also happen when there is mutual respect for each other's opinions, a common work ethic, shared visions and goals, and, of course, enjoyment of one another's company. It is natural for people to immediately think of friends or family members as potential business partners. But you should realize that mixing financial matters in with any relationship often changes the dynamic. It certainly makes the relationship much more serious. Situations that would have been tolerable in a friendship may not be tolerable in a business relationship. Owning a business, people may even exhibit a different side of their personality. You may discover that a friend you thought had a laid-back personality isn't so laissez-faire when it comes to business, but rather a no-nonsense, domineering entrepreneur.

If you do decide to establish a partnership, you should draft an agreement, in writing, that outlines each partner's responsibilities, duties, and percentage of ownership allotted. Not all partnerships need to be split 50/50. In addition to sharing ownership, you will also share the company's debt. In a partnership, you are liable for your own actions plus those of your partners. So if you have a partner with impulsive buying tendencies who purchases a vintage 1912 Chandler & Price platen press for your letterpress company without first asking you, you too will be responsible for paying for that machine. You may want to consider including preemptive clauses in your partnership agreement that discuss potential sticky situations and how they will be handled, should they occur. The agreement should also dictate what to do if one partner wants to withdraw or dissolve the partnership, as well as the proper way to exit the business. For example, you can include a clause that prevents one of the partners from leaving or being relieved of duties without a 30-day advance notice. If that partner is the sole person who knows how to operate the press, you'll need that time to find someone to fill that role. The payout can vary according to the partner's reason for leaving and adherence to the exit policy; this too should be specified in the agreement.

When disputes break out between partners, the root of the problem can often be traced to divergent financial expectations, differing management and work styles, or dissimilar views and goals. A common partnership conflict happens when one partner emerges as the dominant worker or the more talented designer. The partner that is working harder or producing better work can become resentful, especially if she feels that the other partner is riding on her coattails. And when things don't work out, sadly, the price is sometimes friendship. Saying "it's nothing personal, it's just business" is hardly sufficient to save a friendship destroyed by a business divorce. In reality, business is often very personal. You will need to be mindful of this when considering creating a partnership with friends.

Above all, you should know yourself well: If you are fiercely independent with a Type A personality, then don't start or join a partnership. Go solo and save yourself the potential heartache and stress. If you like working with other individuals, you might consider creating or joining a collective so that you could still maintain your business autonomously. If a friend has a great skill to contribute to your venture, consider paying her an hourly wage and skipping the partnership. A solo operation can be just as influential and successful as a group-owned venture. An advantage to being a sole proprietor is that all the work stems from your hands— you get to see firsthand the value of your hard work and, as a happy consequence, reap all the financial rewards for yourself.

What's Your Legal Structure?

The legal structure of your business determines your personal liability and also the taxes you'll have to pay. Structures that limit your liability are C corporations, S corporations, and limited liability companies (LLCs). These structures are usually subject to an annual tax and are filed with the state agencies that handle business filings (e.g., in Illinois, the secretary of state governs these matters). In the event that someone claims your business has harmed them—say, a client suffers a concussion from slipping on spilled ceramic glazing during a visit to your studio—an incorporated structure will protect your individual assets (like your home), and only the assets of the business can be seized. In general, craft businesses that operate out of a home are relatively innocuous and don't deal in inherently risky activities, so creative-business owners usually choose unincorporated options. To know what is best for your company, get a recommendation from a professional, such as an attorney or an accountant who specializes in small businesses. Also, check www.irs.gov for more information.

Sole Proprietorship

This is the route most creative-business owners take when they are going solo, without any employees. This structure doesn't require any formal documentation to say that you are a sole proprietor. Come tax time, all your company's profits and expenses are filed on a form called Schedule C (Profit & Loss from Business).

General Partnership

If your business is a group endeavor, you should have a partnership agreement ironed out that dictates each partner's responsibilities and what percentage each partner owns of the company (see "A Team or Solo Effort," page 40, for more information on this agreement). When you file your taxes, your accountant will file a U.S. Return of Partnership Income.

Limited Partnership

A limited partnership has two levels: general and limited. General partners are responsible for running the business and are liable for the debts and agreements made on behalf of the business. Limited partners are financial backers who have no control over the business but who share in the profits and losses based on what they put into the business.

C Corporation

A C corporation offers limited liability and can be formed with the help of an attorney or accountant. You will need to file paperwork outlining the names of the officers, directors, and shareholders. However, C corporations are subject to double taxation—the company pays taxes on the profits and then each shareholder pays taxes on the money taken from that profit.

S Corporation

An S corporation has the benefit of limited liability without the double taxation issue of a C corporation. It requires hiring an attorney or accountant to file the paperwork for you.

Limited Liability Company (LLC)

LLC is a favorite corporate structure for small business owners. It has limited liability and allows more shareholders than an S corporation. You will need to file an operation agreement with a state agency. Best of all, the LLC doesn't require an attorney or accountant to file.

CHECKLIST: STARTING A BUSINESS

○ Choose a company name

○ File a trademark

○ Decide on company's legal structure

○ File for incorporated status*

○ Apply for a business license

○ Check your location for zoning regulations

○ Apply for a Fictitious Business Name statement (DBA)*

○ Apply for a seller's permit

○ Apply for a Federal Tax ID (EIN)*

○ Discuss home and business liability insurance with an agent

○ Open a business phone line

○ Open a business checking account

○ Get IRS publications for small businesses

○ Get health insurance before you quit your day job

*may not apply to all businesses

Financing Your Business

Unless you've got a seven-figure trust fund or a winning lottery ticket in hand, money might well be an issue as you start your new business. Happily, many craft businesses can be started as sideline careers and don't require a lot of start-up capital. You don't need employees right away, you don't necessarily need to buy a lot of equipment, and you can work from home to keep overhead low. If you need extra funding, you could consider taking a job that directly relates to your business, like becoming a salesperson at a bead shop.

If you plan to work on your business full-time, you will need to take stock of your financial situation. Many business consultants recommend saving up at least a year's worth of living expenses before launching your business. To determine your living expenses, you should accurately calculate your monthly expenses (down to the tin of mints you purchased this afternoon). If your financial reserves match a year's worth of expenses, that's great news—consider a huge financial burden lifted. (Just make sure you act responsibly toward yourself: no dipping into your personal savings for business expenses.) If you don't have enough, or any, savings, you'll have to figure out how you will afford these living expenses. Maybe you need to obtain a loan, cut back on expenses, move back in with your parents, or ask a partner or spouse with sufficient income to pay for the bulk of the bills.

All business-related expenses should come out of your business checking account or be put on the business credit cards. But beware: it's very easy and common to run up debt. Apply for credit cards with low APRs and don't max out your credit cards: stay as debt-lean as possible. The toll on your credit score and your nerves just isn't worth it. You could also secure a small loan from your bank; depending on how much you need, the bank may require a copy of your business plan. Another option is to talk to a lender about securing a small business loan from the federal government's Small Business Administration (SBA). If you ask a friend or family member for the money, clarify the deal before agreeing—are they offering you a loan that accrues interest, or expecting equity in your business with a return on their investment? And remember, even if the loan is coming from family, it's crucial to put the agreement in writing.

In most cases, you'll probably be your own patron—using savings or debt financing. If so, start your business humbly: be prudent with your purchases and keep your overhead very low. Resist the temptation to buy fancy equipment right away or rent a spacious studio. Instead, you should operate with use-what-you've-got principles—work from home and find access to equipment without buying it (e.g., using equipment at a local community arts center). If you commit to expensive items or a lease agreement early on without knowing how much money you will make, you'll have to pay for these things even if business is slow.

In the first year or two, you should expect your business to make very little money, and whatever income you do earn should be reinvested to grow the business. Even though you're the owner, you're often last in line to get paid. So, being a business owner means frugality will be in order. To conserve cash without breaking your creative spirit, look for substitutes for those everyday luxuries: read fashion and lifestyle blogs to curb your magazine habit; turn down takeout and get to know your inner chef; and, of course, as a crafty individual, you should make gifts instead of buying them. Little savings such as these can go a long way.

BETH WEINTRAUB, San Francisco, California
Etched Metal Modular Art

Despite having a creative job sculpting body armor for the San Francisco Opera, Beth Weintraub still yearned for a career that was more expressive of her inner voice. Longing to spend more time doing printmaking, she set off to become an independent artist. In the beginning, the business (creating metal artwork and prints made from hand-painted etchings) was off to a slow start, grossing only $11,000 in the first year. A transformation took place when she came up with the novel idea of selling her etched metal plates as pieces of modular art along with the prints generated from those plates, turning both ends of the printmaking process into a salable product. (Imagine if a painter sold his paintbrushes as well as the canvas as works of art!) Eight years later, she has three part-time employees and rakes in enough in annual sales to allow her to buy a coveted 4,500-square-foot warehouse studio in San Francisco. Beth's company is a testament to the importance of honing your business acumen. So take note: you don't need to starve for your art.

How did you prepare yourself to start a business?

Before I started my business, I took a 14-week course through the Renaissance Entrepreneurship Center in San Francisco. It introduced simple business concepts and how to create a business plan. The course showed how to calculate the cost to make any product, whether a piece of art, a muffin, or even a song! And more importantly, I learned how much you have to sell in order to make a living. I really learned how to think like a businessperson to promote my art.

Do you produce your art yourself or do you get help?

In the beginning, I did nearly all the work. Occasionally, I would need help with tasks like drilling holes or something. I used to make these etched metal, square, tetrahedron bowls, where I would be drilling 10,000 holes for a week! When I had knee surgery two and half years ago, I was out for three months. And it became apparent that I needed an assistant to pick up the slack. So I hired an assistant who helps me with the modular art pieces I do now. Even if you're hurt or sick, you still have to run the business. That experience taught me how to let go of parts of the business.

How did you go about setting your wholesale minimum requirement for your artwork?

I have a three-piece minimum. I designed my art so that it looks best in a group. Each modular piece introduces a different shape or form so that, when they're grouped together, the eye is tickled. When buyers think of buying just one, they realize it just doesn't look as good—so they end up buying at least three to make it work. This works great for the galleries and retailers because they end up selling three pieces at a time. I make sure that I send them language to train their staff so that they're versed on how to sell it. This type of hand-holding, or educating people on your art, really increases sales.

What trade shows do you participate in?

I've been exhibiting at the New York International Gift Fair twice a year since 2001, and I do the California Gift Show in Los Angeles occasionally. It's funny because no one attends a gift show intending to buy fine art, but, believe me, they end up walking out with an order for a few of my pieces. In the past, I participated in the American Craft Council Show in Baltimore and the Rosen Show in Philadelphia. I wasn't prepared for the retail part of the Baltimore show, and I also realized that I didn't want to deal too much with the end user, so I didn't do that show again. I've also done a show in London called Top Drawer. It wasn't a smashing success, but I walked away with international connections.

With increased sales and popularity often comes copying. Has anyone knocked off your work?

Yes, a mass-merchandising home furnishings company is offering etched metal art that looks like my work—they didn't even bother to change the size or the type of illustration. It's such a cheap and bad version of my work. People have contacted me asking if I was working with that » company. It really just cheapens my brand. Right now I'm working on this issue with a lawyer who mentioned that it is not necessarily a copyright infringement issue, but might instead be a trade dress issue—the company is trespassing on my brand.

It really sounds like you're living the dream, owning a warehouse studio. How does it feel to own a building dedicated to your art and business? And what was the process like, getting an SBA loan to finance it?

It's really great. I think every artist fantasizes about having their own warehouse to do their art. I know I've been dreaming about it for a long time. I'm not a spiritual type, but I really think visualization works. If you can visualize it, you can work toward it. I had been working out of a live/work apartment and had frankly outgrown it. I was renting other spaces in the building for additional work space. Then I thought, why not get a warehouse and live and work there! I found this run-down brewery in the Mission District. It's 4,500 square feet with three stories. It needed a lot of work: engineering, plumbing, painting, you name it. I pursued an SBA loan instead of a commercial loan because it required 10% down instead of 30%. And the process was much easier than I thought it would be! I think it helped that my business was established with an eight-year track record. I had an accounting software program that generated my profit and loss statements as well as sales figures, so those were easy to provide. I think the banker was just blown away at how organized and prepared I was—that was probably surprising coming from an artist.

Record Keeping

For most small business operations, being a bookkeeper is one of the least exciting, but one of the most important, hats you must wear. It is not a job to take lightly. As managing business finances can be tedious and time-consuming, you should create an efficient record-keeping system from the very beginning. Bookkeeping means keeping complete and accurate records of your business's income and expenses. You need to be a paper hoarder—keeping copies of invoices, bills, checks, and receipts and filing them in an organized manner. In addition to creating a paper filing system, everything needs to be logged as well. When you get a parking receipt at a trade show, it should be inputted into record-keeping books or software and then filed. You also need to keep track of business-related mileage that you've driven.

There are several ways to maintain your books: the old-school way (i.e., writing things down in ledgers) or the technology-age way (i.e., using an accounting management system like QuickBooks or Peachtree). The latter is the preferred method for most small businesses, as it can help you create and track unpaid invoices, monitor purchases and inventory, and print checks. But bookkeeping software can run you a couple hundred

For most small business operations, being a bookkeeper is one of the least exciting, but one of the most important, hats you must wear.

dollars, not to mention the software is made for accountants and can be quite sophisticated. In addition to learning the software, you will need to learn accounting lingo. An alternative is to hire an accountant to set your company up in an accounting program and then give you a tutorial.

If you plan to manage finances without a computer accounting program, you will still need to have basic accounting know-how, such as how to create appropriate income and expense accounts. You can take workshops or classes on small business operations to help you understand things like deductible expenses and to help you manage record-keeping. It's fine to start your business using handwritten invoices and sales receipts; just make sure you make copies for your files. You will need to be especially disciplined and organized in regard to your accounts receivable (or outstanding invoices); make sure you have a reliable method for keeping track of who has paid and who hasn't. And remember that if you're confused about bookkeeping, it's best to consult with an accountant before tax time; backtracking over an entire year's worth of income, expenses, and associated paperwork can be a horrendous headache.

TALK TO YOUR LOVED ONES

Owning a business changes your schedule and your lifestyle: you'll essentially have less free time and, possibly, less money. It is important to discuss this with important people in your life, like your spouse, domestic partner, roommates, and children. You also might want to consider having the important people in your life involved in some aspect of your business so that you aren't isolated from them too often, and so they feel like they share in the success of your company.

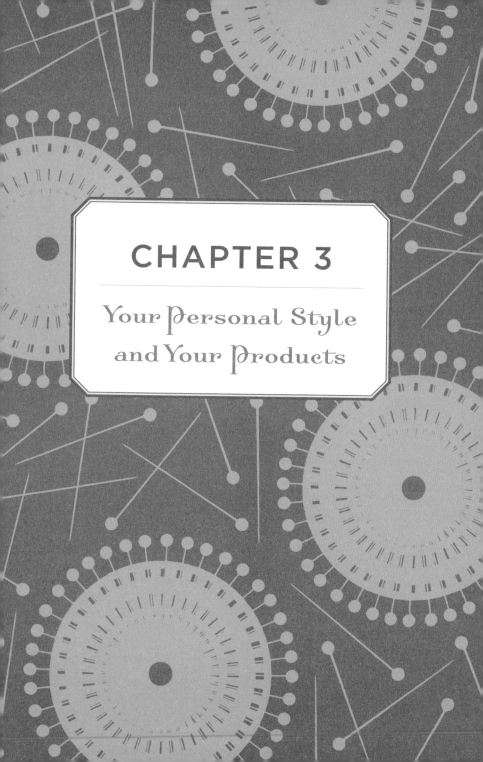

CHAPTER 3

Your Personal Style and Your Products

With your newly established creative confidence (and technical business details conveniently out of the way), it's time to bring your style into focus. Your company's debut product line should capture the eye and imagination of potential customers. Once you enter the game, you will face competition with more experience and an existing customer base, so it helps to come in with your creative guns blazing. There are plenty of mediocre items on the market; make your product one that leaves a lasting, positive impression. Your task now is to create products, whether a cohesive collection or a hodgepodge of goodies. The common thread running through your products should be a signature aesthetic, design, technique, and/or illustration style. Your goal should be to make your products and your brand immediately identifiable.

Keeping It Real

Joining a creative industry does not mean you need to subscribe to preconceptions of how a creative individual should look, act, or think! Refrain from running to your nearest Salvation Army for vintage duds, buying film-school specs, or getting an avant-garde coif to create an appearance that screams *artist* with a capital "A" (or *hipster* with a lowercase "h," for that matter). You don't need a particular look to be accepted by the community. The same applies to what you create; it should always be an authentic expression of you. You might be tempted to hold back on a project in order to fit the current trends, or perhaps you feel your product is not hip, sexy, flashy, or witty enough. If you're out of step with the trends,

Some people will like your product and some people won't, but the most important thing is that you like it.

don't betray your voice by apologizing for it or by trying to fabricate a new one. Your efforts to get in with the cool kids will probably fall flat. Plus, in the end, you will feel more satisfied if you stay true to yourself. Perhaps your style isn't out in the marketplace yet, and that will become your niche. Some people will like your product and some people won't, but the most important thing is that you like it.

Creative Mission Statement

In order to stay focused and keep your projects personal, it helps to develop a creative mission statement. When you are clear about your goals, it will be easier to work toward achieving them. A creative mission statement is essentially a verbalized belief system, enunciating your motivations, values, and vision. When you bring these elements into your projects, you'll have a greater sense of confidence, fulfillment, and purpose. Rereading your creative mission statement is also a way to double-check that your current projects are charged with your personality and adequately satisfy your ideals. Formulating your statement will require you to be introspective and delve into your creative urges and callings.

Visualize the type of products that you value and dream of and that inspire you. A creative mission can be a group of statements. For example,

My creative mission is:

※ To craft as many products as I can by hand

※ To design products that don't follow trends

※ To find beauty in the mundane

※ To be slow and conscientious when I create products

※ To create products that show an appreciation for old-world craftsmanship

Company Identity

Along the same lines as drafting your creative mission statement is the task of determining your company identity. By creating an identity or image, you are communicating a message about your company; this is often called branding. Your brand is an idea, not just your logo, colors, stationery, and packaging—though those elements will reflect your brand. For example, Jonathan Adler has branded his company as eclectic and modern with a sense of humor, whereas Ralph Lauren has branded his company as preppy and classic. How would you like others to describe your company? And what feelings and thoughts do you want brought to mind?

You should formulate an image that reflects your company's personality but that also will be appealing to your potential customers.

To establish a brand, think about what you want your company to represent and how that can be relayed through elements ranging from the photographs on your Web site to your products and packaging. Consistency is key. If your logo is a playful cartoon dog and your Web site is as serious as a commercial bank, what will people make of your products? What message will be derived from your brand? Do you want the tone to be serious or whimsical? You should formulate an image that reflects your company's personality but that will also be appealing to your potential customers. Getting feedback from friends and colleagues is an important step toward ensuring that the intended feelings and tone are being accurately communicated by your brand.

DENYSE SCHMIDT, Bridgeport, Connecticut
Quilts

Coming from a family of craftspeople and learning to sew at the age of eight, Denyse Schmidt can thank a lifetime of practice and craftsmanship for her runaway success. In 1996, she emerged as the most buzzed-about indie designer when she launched her line of quilts at the International Contemporary Furniture Fair (ICFF). For the next five years, evenings *chez* Schmidt were anything but relaxing, as she juggled a full-time job and her creative business. What else can you expect when you're knee-deep in revolutionizing the world of quilting? By introducing a clean, modern sensibility that challenged many prevailing notions, Denyse Schmidt made it cool to quilt again.

What is your design process like?

I start with a hand-drawn sketch. Then I use the computer and redraw my sketch in Adobe Illustrator to bring the drawing to scale. The challenge is finding a way for other people to help make my quilt designs in a way that retains the feeling of the initial sketch—because there aren't any straight lines there. Charles and Ray Eames were into production to make great design available to a wide audience. I like the challenge of figuring out how to make things that have an individual, one-off feel using mass production.

I put colors together in a very visceral way. I don't think about it a whole lot. We have a lot of learned ideas about color—about what goes together. But I think people should trust their instincts. People sometimes say, "I don't know anything about color!" But you do—you know what you like and what you respond to.

How long were you doing your quilt business part-time?

I was working full-time at another job when I started the business. Over the next four years I ran my business while gradually working part-time at this other job. People are quick to think that you are an overnight success. They assume that if you're in magazines and on TV, you're just coasting along and you've got it figured out. You think I worry about paying bills? You bet I do! Craft-based businesses do not come easily—it's a matter of figuring out how to make it work for you.

How do you make the quilts?

I have three collections. The Couture Quilts are my signature line. These are pieced in my studio, and hand-quilted by Amish quilters. Most of the designs do not have patterns—we cut and sew the quilt tops together in an improvisational way. Each Couture Quilt takes at least six months to complete. The second collection is Denyse Schmidt Works. These quilts are also pieced in my studio, then machine-quilted locally. The third collection is licensed through a manufacturer in India, and is my most affordable quilt line. I design the quilts, specify fabrics, and help direct the overall brand and strategy. The manufacturer produces all the quilts and packaging, and does all the distribution and sales.

How did you connect with the Amish? How do you go about working them?

Working with them was an easy process. They're set up as a cottage industry. I was looking in the back of a quilting magazine and there are all these ads for Amish hand-quilting, so anyone can find those resources. I work with someone who is not Amish, who oversees the process. She has about 30 to 40 women working for her. Since the Amish don't use modern technology to communicate, working with middlemen makes the process easier. It's been an interesting partnership.

How did you go about finding a manufacturer in India?

Garnet Hill approached me about doing some designs for them. And I basically told them I wanted to meet with their manufacturer in case I wanted to work with them on my own someday. The manufacturer was Sarita Handa in India. Although I feel strongly about domestic production, most consumers aren't able to support that. Having some of my product line produced overseas means I can reach a range of market segments, and each part supports the rest. »

Quilts seem like a difficult product to price. Did you struggle with pricing them in the beginning?

Quilts *are* difficult to price. There is a long-standing tradition of underselling them. Since quilt-making is typically a hobby, people don't really price their hours appropriately. That said, when priced correctly, quilts are expensive products. Neither I nor my friends could afford the quilts I was making. In the beginning, I sold the couture quilts through stores, but they proved difficult for retailers to sell because of the price, which runs from $2,500 to $6,000. So I no longer offer them at wholesale discount.

What elements do you think contributed to the success of your business?

An idea that was very instrumental in launching my business came from a friend who wanted to change her career. She suggested that we get together once a month to meet. It was the beginning of what we called the "Girls Group," and ten years later we're still doing it. The intent of the group was to help support each other and provide a sounding board for whatever we needed to accomplish—mostly revolving around our business careers.

I make very personal and conscious choices with what I design, where it's sold, and even where we make charitable donations. And it shows. Nothing is arbitrary. If your work is close to your heart and important to you, it comes across somehow in an intangible sense of uniqueness and honesty.

Starting the Ideation Process

Depending on how you work and the types of projects you have in mind, the ideation process will vary. Inspiration comes in different packages; sometimes it's a complete idea, other times it's merely a seed. Don't put pressure on yourself to generate groundbreaking products every time. Your goal should be to make a product that satisfies you and takes advantage of your creative strengths. As you design your product, remember that you don't have to make something drastically different from what's out there, just different enough that it presents a new angle or an innovative improvement. Sometimes it is that one small detail that sets a product apart from the rest—like an apron that closes with a belt buckle. You can even think about simplifying objects: maybe the apron doesn't need anything to close it! Whatever the product is, it should always fall within the realm of making an original contribution to the world.

It helps to start slowly, beginning with a single project and thinking about the small details instead of thinking of the object or collection as a whole. Follow your vision, even if it doesn't make sense to other people. Try not to make any practical concessions in the first stages of product creation: don't worry about your materials budget or your capacity to apply hundreds of rhinestones. As design is an iterative process, you can always edit later. Fully document your ideation process by making notes

Since no single product will please everyone, your collection should vary in purpose, price, and production.

(e.g., listing colors and materials), sketching, and creating prototype models to see the evolution of your work. Don't be too quick to write off your mistakes. If you change your perspective, mistakes can be opportunities. You never know when your subconscious is trying to offer a helping hand in your design process. Also, give your projects time to develop. Sleep on your ideas or take a couple days away from them to give yourself time to review it all with a fresh eye.

If you are creating a collection, remember that the best ones are the most focused, revolving around a single concept or source of inspiration: perhaps you want to explore blue and green color combinations in your jewelry or use floral silhouettes in your bedding and pillows. You will also want to find the middle ground between having a collection that is one-note and one that covers too many ideas. Collections should also aim to be memorable from start to finish. There shouldn't be mind-blowing products mixed in with some that are obviously filler. There should be a consistent aesthetic, stylistic vocabulary, and design rigor that runs through all your work.

Since no single product will please everyone, your collection should vary in purpose, price, and production. Customers like having a variety of products to choose from and tend to look around your Web site or booth more when there is a greater selection of goods. After all, if you only make belts, how many can one person buy? But if you make belts and bags, you may have just doubled your sale from each customer. People will come to you with a variety of budgets, so products that range from low to high will capture clients at all points along the spectrum. Last and most important, if you will be making a majority of your items by hand, they can't all be labor-intensive. A good number of items should require none to very little of your labor—these can be your bread-and-butter pieces. Otherwise, this craft you call your labor of love may suddenly become *very* laborious.

Capture Your Ideas

Whether your mind is forever churning out ideas or your inspiration comes in occasional spurts of brilliance, you need to be ready to seize these creative opportunities. You could be in line at the grocery store, on your way to pick up the kids from school, or curling up in bed ready for some shut-eye when the little lightbulb turns on in your head. It's helpful to carry a small journal, index cards, or a notebook to capture the ideas before they evaporate. And leave one by your nightstand, too. Sometimes your mind has to be stimulated in order for ideas to materialize. If that's the case, you can act as a catalyst in your ideation process. If you're unsure about your creative inclinations, you want to embark with a clean slate, or your mind needs a little nudge to generate ideas, start a journal and fill it with right-brained activities to open your mind—remember not to edit yourself or judge your work. Here are some ways to jump-start your imagination:

₨ Make daily observations, using all five senses, of things around you, including textures, sounds, movements, and colors.

₨ Break from creative patterns or habits. For example, if you're typically a verbal person, try drawing, or if you're a visual thinker, try writing.

₨ Let intuition guide your hand, and doodle without purpose.

₨ Let your unconscious ideas flow, and write words in a stream of consciousness.

₨ Cull ideas from every possible source: the street, music, art, advertising, overheard conversations, etc.

₨ Read books and magazines. Take notes on images you see or stories you've read.

₨ Go on creative field trips. Take photographs and place found items in your journal.

Setting Goals

Once you've started your business, you'll need to set goals on a weekly basis. Making a weekly goal sheet and putting your plans in writing will make your business plans feel very real. It's best to diversify by mixing easy and hard goals. Easy goals can be things like attending a craft fair, picking a place in your home to set up your business, making a list of projects you'd like to make, or getting together with a person in your creative network to bounce ideas.

Your harder goals will likely either revolve around the business end of your craft or involve completing craft projects. It takes discipline to finish the harder goals, so try to subdivide your tasks into smaller, more edible bites (e.g., call the bank and ask for an appointment to discuss opening a business account). You can check off each mini-accomplishment that brings you closer to completing your weekly goals. Although a certain amount of stress is needed to keep your motivation level high, too much stress (as in setting too many goals) can work against you, so be realistic about how many things you can accomplish in a given day or week. And it doesn't hurt to approach every task, however small, with joie de vivre.

Market Research

Creating a product that embodies your creative voice isn't exactly like formulating a new soft drink to satisfy millions of people. It's more personal than that. But at the same time, you may not be an artist in the traditional sense—putting single, one-of-a-kind pieces out there that merely satisfy your imagination. You are placing a creative commodity on the market for group consumption. You need to make things that people will want to buy.

To give your products the best chance possible, your assignment is to figure out the buying public's interests. The first and easiest step is to go to a bookstore or library and pick up craft or lifestyle magazines and see what kinds of products and trends are garnering editorial coverage. Next, visit local stores that would likely carry your type of products, to see what buyers are placing on their shelves. Lastly, get to know your future competitors by attending trade shows and craft fairs. In your research, pay particular attention to designers engaged in the same craft as you and make notes on the following things:

❧ What types of products are already out in the market? Which areas are particularly saturated? Conversely, what products did you not see?

❧ What trends (product, style, material, color, or otherwise) did you notice? Would you follow any of these trends?

❧ How many booths/tables are essentially selling the same type of product or have a similar aesthetic? How many share your aesthetic?

❧ Was there a designer whose products struck you on an emotional level? Why?

❦ Was there a designer whose booth/table was particularly popular? Why do you think people were drawn to that designer?

❦ What was the wholesale or retail pricing range for goods you may be interested in launching yourself?

Attending trade shows and craft fairs is a great way to get inspiration, ideas, and an improved understanding of the marketplace. These trips can also be reassuring, especially if you notice that your aesthetic or particular product isn't popular yet. Whenever you attend one of these events, try your best not to make it obvious that you're mining for ideas or information. Designers are pretty perceptive about people who are doing some visual shopping (or shoplifting, however you look at it). Craft fairs are the easiest shows to attend since they are open to the public. (See "Craft Fair Revival," page 104.) It's easy to survey the scene: all you have to do is act like you're shopping or, better yet, actually buy some goodies in the name of market research.

Attending trade shows and craft fairs is a great way to get inspiration, ideas, and an improved understanding of the marketplace.

Trade shows, where vendors sell their wares to retailers, are generally open to the trade (and press) only, which means you'll have to prove that you are a legitimate business. You do this by showing documentation, such as your Web site URL, a photo of your storefront, a business card, a resale license, and/or copies of recent invoices from your vendors. You can register online or in person, or you can contact trade show management directly. If you tell them that you're interested in exhibiting in future shows, they may give or sell you a guest pass. When you arrive at the show, you'll see booth after booth of designers, all aiming to do the same thing: sell. Luckily, there is a method to navigating the seemingly endless rows of manufacturers. As trade shows sample every taste imaginable, a majority of the exhibitors will be of little interest to you. Usually vendors are organized into themed sections; you can figure out which ones apply to you when you get there, or you can get a list of vendors to study before the show. (For more information, see "Trade Shows," page 121.)

When you enter a company's booth, someone will take a look at your badge to see your name, the company you represent, and, most important, whether you are a buyer, an exhibitor, or the press. Depending on how chatty the company's representatives are or how busy the booth is, several things could happen:

1 The representative could hit you up with a barrage of questions (Where is your store? Is it online or brick-and-mortar? What do you sell?).

2 The representative might allow you to look around without question.

OR

3 You might slip completely unnoticed into the booth.

Your comfort level will dictate whether you study the booth while being elusive or mention that you are a new designer thinking about participating in a trade show one day. In either case, if you want to get copies of line sheets (which list product prices) and catalogs from booths you visit, it will be a little tricky, unless they are lying around in plain view. Most manufacturers are very guarded about giving out their information. Normally, companies only give copies of their catalogs and line sheets if you leave your business card in exchange. And if you don't own a shop, a business card might not be sufficient. So bring a notebook to jot down company names and look up their Web sites when you get home. Just don't take notes while you're in the booths!

The distance between where you are now and where you want to be may become instantly apparent.

Attending a craft fair or trade show can easily eat up an entire day, and you may come home a jumbled ball of mixed feelings. You might have an adrenaline rush and a flurry of inspirational ideas running through your head, or you might feel like you've stuck a pin in your creative bubble by comparing yourself to some of the creative businesses you've just visited. The distance between where you are now and where you want to be may become instantly apparent. It's okay to feel a little jealous or envious but know that these types of feelings can work against you if you let them linger. Instead of feeling inadequate, channel that energy into working harder on your craft. Those designers were in your shoes once and had to work hard at it, too.

WOOL & HOOP, Marfa, Texas
Crewel Kits

Katherine Shaughnessy's passion for embroidery is evident, from her childhood sewing projects to achieving a master's degree in Fiber Arts. After searching for embroidery kits featuring a specific technique called crewel, she realized that there weren't any on the market with a contemporary flair befitting her style. She began incubating an idea to design crewel kits with mod flourishes and organic geometric shapes, but the plan lay dormant for several years. Like many first-time business owners, her first "products" were gifts to her nieces and nephews. Despite being advised by well-meaning friends that the kits would be very unprofitable, Katherine forged ahead with her plan, at the urging of her husband. She quickly learned about the semisecret world of craft, the struggles of being a business owner far from the big city, and the delight of having her own embroidery book published.

When did you realize that craft could be a profitable business venture?

I think, to most people, craft products don't look very profitable at all. I had doubts myself and was very hesitant to start my own business. But after attending my first trade show, the Craft and Hobby Association (CHA) Show in Dallas, which is a wholesale, business-to-business show, it really changed the way I thought about craft. You don't really know how big the craft world is until you attend a trade show. It was truly an awakening for me. There's a whole craft culture out there that most people are unaware of.

What was the response to your products when you exhibited at trade shows?

I'd never done a trade show before Dallas, but I quickly learned that you have to be very careful at trade shows. There was this one guy who was trying to steal one of my kits—and even pretended not to speak English! At the Dallas show, I got great responses from publications but not from retailers. It seemed that everyone at this fair was looking for scrapbooking-related stuff. One of the good things that came from the show was that publishers approached me for book deals. That was totally unexpected. In November 2005, I released *The New Crewel,* a book featuring crewel projects. I still can't believe how quickly it all happened.

How have you marketed your business?

I've been fortunate so far in that I really haven't done any legwork to get the press I've gotten. DailyCandy wrote us up in an article two years ago and I sold hundreds of kits. It was insane! From that, I think some retailers and other members of the press learned about my kits, giving Wool & Hoop the momentum it needed. My business has been featured in the *Wall Street Journal,* of all places, and in *ReadyMade.*

What has been your experience searching for vendors to produce your kits?

It's actually a nightmare trying to find vendors. For one thing, I live in a small Texas town where you don't have the luxury of going to Kinko's for quick printing. It's almost like island living out here. There isn't a selection of vendors to choose from and you're essentially at everybody's mercy. The local printer I was working with just disappeared! When you're searching for vendors, you have to know that you will definitely hit a lot of dead ends.

What's next for you?

I would like to operate strictly as a wholesale business and work solely with retailers so that I can spend more time designing more kits than filling orders coming in through the Web site. Outside of making kits, I would also like to provide supplies for crewelwork, like linen, wool, needles, and hoops, so that individuals can make their own designs.

Trend Watch

Even though the world is an infinite repository of inspiration and ideas, inevitably a group of unrelated designers adopt a *de rigueur* style—a specific material (felt, plywood); a process (laser-cut, letterpress); a motif (birds, skulls, flora); a color scheme (chocolate brown and baby blue); or a product (iPod cozy, buttons)—and introduce it to the marketplace with

As a general rule of thumb, your work should aspire to timelessness and staying power.

alarming frequency. It's good to know what trends are in, but you don't need to jump on any bandwagons; choose which trends fall in line with your vision and which do not. Be wary and check your local superstores, since mass production can hasten the demise of a trend. As a general rule of thumb, your work should aspire to timelessness and staying power. Although the goal of your business is to make money, if you chase trends simply to turn a buck, you'll run the risk of burning out quickly. The best trends will be the ones that you initiate, not follow.

Copying Your Creative Muses

Since you will be exposed to a wealth of talent out there, it's important that we address a common problem in the creative business community: copying. The phrase "Imitation is the sincerest form of flattery" is sometimes just a polite excuse for plagiarizing someone else's work. When something is successful for someone else, it may be tempting to emulate that work or those techniques. Truly, there is nothing wrong with being inspired by the work of your creative muses. In fact, imitating a pro is one way to learn certain techniques. But copying should be a stepping-stone in your developmental process, not an end product. In other words, copying should be a private exercise, not a business practice. If you find someone's work inspiring, apply the spirit of it to your work while maintaining your individual style. Do you love a product line that marries unexpected techniques like pottery and sewing? Challenge yourself to use a different set of contrasting techniques, such as knitting and woodwork, in your own designs. Your work should merely allude to that of other artists, not mimic it.

The last thing you should want to do is degrade your own creative wit and integrity by making an ersatz remake of someone else's design. Taking pieces of someone else's design cannot be considered an original work either. Even though the less-than-design-literate public won't be able to differentiate between the original and its appropriator, don't assume that your copying will go unnoticed. The design and craft community is quite close-knit—word gets around fast. Plus, with a little thing known as patent or copyright law, you could be reprimanded by the original designer or, worse yet, her attorney. If nothing else, you wouldn't want to anger the karmic gods—if you steal someone else's ideas, know that there's someone out there waiting to snatch up yours.

Using Images and Patterns

As a designer, you should exercise caution when you reproduce existing images or patterns in your designs. For images, be sure to check for copyrights and verify that they are royalty-free (meaning that the creator of the image gives up future rights to the image for a fee). You can buy royalty-free clip art online or in books. Don't assume that something you find in an old or out-of-print book is necessarily in the public domain. And even making small changes to a pattern or illustration does not make it an original work—if it looks similar, that may be sufficient for a lawsuit.

If you sew, knit, or crochet, be careful about creating objects for sale based on a pattern you purchased. For example, most old, traditional quilt patterns are not copyrighted and can be resold, but a cross-stitch guide from a magazine or dress patterns and embroidery kits purchased at a fabric store are meant for personal consumption only. They cannot be used to make a wholesale or retail line of products. In addition, copyright laws also cover illustrations and patterns on fabric. For example, Amy Butler Design's Web site clearly states that her fabric is for noncommercial use only. If you plan to create an item using an existing patterned fabric, contact the manufacturer or designer about any limitations on the use of the fabric or ask for permission to reuse it.

As a designer, you should exercise caution when you reproduce existing images or patterns in your designs.

If your business involves collage in any way, you will need to be very careful. The nature of collage is derivative. However, only the copyright owner has the legal right to create a new version or derivative of their work. So, to be safe, if you want to include someone else's work in your collage, get permission or clearance, even if it is only for a photograph from a magazine or a map ripped from your *Thomas Guide*. Naturally, there are elements you can include that are considered "fair use," like vintage 1920s photographs you purchased through eBay. Collage is copyrightable as long as the work is significantly different from any other single work. Filing for copyright is often not a problem, as it combines many layers of elements to create a new whole work, but consult an attorney to be sure your work isn't vulnerable to lawsuit.

Packaging

Though packaging is the last step in designing your product, it is an integral step and often requires as much planning and thought as it took to put together your lip balm collection. However, while many independent designers cosset their creations, some fall short when packaging them. In their haste to release a product, some eschew any packaging at all, while others affix a quick label or fall back too easily on tried-and-true methods. The result is often a mismatched product and package pair, like a sophisticated product wearing clumsy clothes or, worse yet, a fancy product lacking any garments at all. Good packaging can enhance your product's value, strengthen your brand, and draw attention to the item as it sits on a store's shelf.

Sometimes you can sell something based on good packaging alone, but who wants something that's all packaging and no substance? You'll want to strike a balance between product and packaging. Packaging doesn't have to be expensive; it just needs to look professional. Your packaging can be as simple as using remnant fabric to make hangtags and stamping them with your logo or, simpler still, making clever labels for your candles using an ink-jet printer. If your goods are handmade, you can include a tiny sheet explaining the story behind your company and your production methods in the packaging. When applicable, you should include information on how to take care of your product, listing materials used and washing instructions. Your goods should always be marked with your company name and/or logo, as well as your URL, whenever possible.

Evaluating Your Products

Once you've designed a product, the next step is to evaluate it. The first question you should ask yourself is "Would I buy this?" It's so easy to get caught up in the designing of fanciful goodies that sometimes it doesn't dawn on you to consider whether or not you would actually purchase the items yourself. Next, ask yourself "What type of person would buy this item?" Realistically, unless you're inventing a new toothpaste, the answer to this question will not be "everyone." Think like a marketing executive: Is it for men? Women? People who love the Victorian era? Once you know your niche market, review your goods to see if they aptly speak to that group of consumers. Good questions to consider are: "Are there similar products already on the market?" and "How well can this product stand up to the competition?"

Lastly, ask yourself "Am I happy with how the product looks and how it is made?" You will want to have a reputation for making quality, well-made goods. You wouldn't want your block-printed pillow cover to fade in the initial washing or your flower hairpins to fall apart after one use. Products must stand up to normal usage. So create several samples of your scarves and give them to your friends gratis, mail a sample wedding invitation to yourself, and wash a couple of your tie-dyed pillowcases, to see what happens. The design process doesn't end just because the job looks complete.

After you've evaluated your work, it's time to ask others to look with a critical eye. Ask individuals whose opinion you value highly and who have some awareness about the market for your products—your dad, who doesn't know a thing about removable wall decals, is probably not a good choice. Opening the door to criticism can be unnerving and awakens those insecurities you thought you had put to bed. It'll be up to you to figure out which comments have merit and are well-meaning and which are manipulative potshots aimed at your creative confidence—hopefully none if you're talking to the right people. Don't try to defend your work and quell any dissenters; sometimes you have to set aside your ego to heed the wisdom others can provide. Go back to the drawing board if necessary to work out any kinks. When at last you have a product design that you believe in and feel your target market would prefer over the competition, it's time to move forward.

SEPARATED AT BIRTH

Sometimes another designer's style is so in line with yours that you can almost swear you were separated at birth. Inasmuch as you think you're doing something original, there may be someone else out there in the world doing something similar simultaneously. All of a sudden, they come out with a product or style that you've been working feverishly on. The only difference is that your "twin" came out with it first. Since inspiration does not occur in a vacuum, we're all largely a product of the same influences, and different people often reach similar ends. When this strange phenomenon happens, after kicking yourself in the pants for not putting your goods out first, you should consider whether to launch your goods or remake them so that they vary widely from your competitor's goods.

Protecting Your Work

In the hypercompetitive craft and design arena, designers need to be aggressive about protecting their work. The two main means of acquiring the fullest protection of the law for your intellectual property are filing for patents and registering copyrights. Patents are issued by the United States Patent and Trademark Office and protect inventions and discoveries. If you patent a new bracelet clasp, you have the exclusive right to make, use, or sell that clasp for 20 years. Two types of patents that concern crafters are utility patents, covering "new" (meaning the invention was not previously available to the public anywhere in the world) and "useful" (meaning the invention works) processes and improvements, and design

> Once you own the copyright, you have the exclusive right to reproduce and distribute the work or to create derivative works.

patents, covering new, original, and ornamental design for a manufactured item. To learn more about filing a patent, see the "Internet Resources" section on page 156 or speak to a patent attorney.

Copyright protects original works of authorship, including artistic works like illustrations, patterns, and photographs, as well as the design and content of your Web site. (Sadly, an idea cannot be copyrighted.) The moment you draw some lines or snap a photograph, your work is technically copyrighted by law, but you should still take the extra, and very easy, steps to officially register with the U.S. Copyright Office. Once you own the copyright, you have the exclusive right to reproduce and distribute the work or to create derivative works. Additionally, to underscore ownership of your work, you should place a copyright line on every piece you make. The standard "Copyright © 2006 by John Doe. All rights reserved." should work just fine.

When filing for copyright, you can often send a group of work, rather than sending it piecemeal, and pay one flat fee. And contrary to urban legend, mailing yourself a copy of your design through the U.S. Postal Service is not a proper method for securing copyright protection. There is no substitution for registering the work with the U.S. Copyright Office. Visit www.copyright.gov to find the current fee schedule and instructions on how to get the application process started. Of course, taking the steps to register a copyright or file a patent will not necessarily prevent someone from making something similar, but it can give you legal protection should someone outright reproduce your work or make something uncannily similar without your permission.

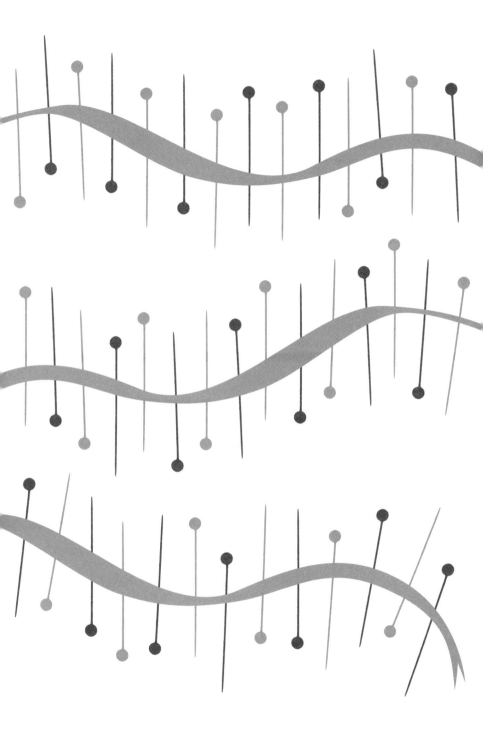

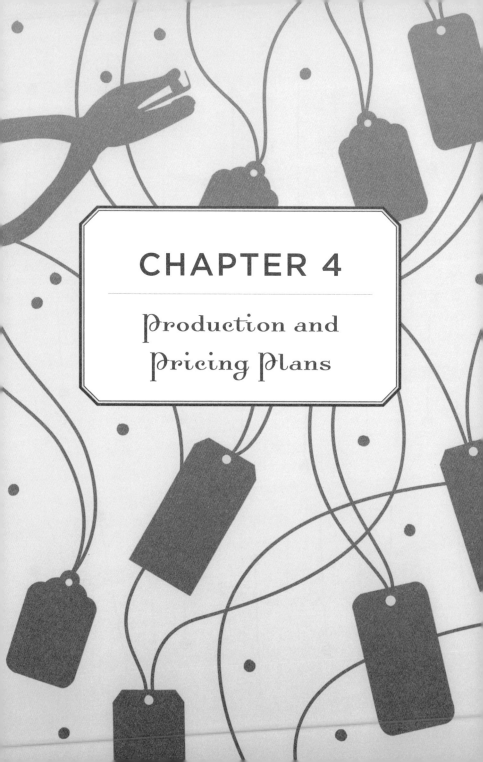

CHAPTER 4

Production and
Pricing Plans

With supplies from your local bead store, you've assembled the prototype for an ebony wood and sterling-silver choker. *Gosh,* you wonder, *how can I make 10, or even 100, of these at a decent profit? Where can I buy these flat sterling-silver links at wholesale cost? And, short of learning how to whittle wood, how can I get these ebony wood beads customized into the shape of a bulbous kidney bean?* This chapter will show you the various methods of finding that needle-in-the-haystack supplier—a bead importer in Lincoln, Massachusetts, or a button manufacturer in Hanoi, Vietnam. After you've sourced materials and found manufacturers, you face the difficult task of pricing. How much should you charge for your necklaces? A formula is a good starting point. But pricing is more than that—it's also about creating a perceived value for your goods. If your jewelry is indeed as special as you think it is, it should have a price tag to match.

Sourcing Raw Materials and Vendors

It might be convenient for newbie craft businesses to pay retail prices for materials at a local craft store. But doing so will make the price of your goods too exorbitant or, conversely, reduce your profit margin considerably. As a business, it is best to order materials and services from vendors that offer wholesale pricing. But how do you find wholesale suppliers and service providers?

As with most things, finding a vendor requires elbow grease and a little bit of luck. There isn't a hidden technique, book, or Web site that will help you locate all the vendors you'll ever need. And although you may be tempted, it's best to refrain from asking another designer for his sources—even if you've become friends. Creative-business owners work hard to find their vendors, so it's not fair to ask them to give away their hard-earned sources. The first step many designers take is to do a Google search. Unfortunately, the road between typing "vegetable-based ink printer" and actually finding one can be littered with rotten links. One reliable source is the Thomas Register of American Manufacturers, which has a Web site you can search, books you can look through (check your local library), and CDs you can order. Some of the best sources are trade shows—where you can actually meet vendors in person as well as see and touch samples of their work or materials. There are trade shows that focus on specific crafts (like jewelry design or soap-making) or materials (like textiles or beads and gems). See the "Internet Resources" section on page 156 for trade show suggestions.

It can take contacting several manufacturers or vendors to find the right one for you. The first few e-mails or conversations will familiarize you with the terminology and proper questions for your particular industry. When you approach your first offset-lithography printing vendor, who throws out words like *gripper, plate, registration,* and *bleed,* you're bound to sound amateurish and, as a result, receive higher quotes for materials or services than an experienced craftsperson would. Although it's tempting, never go with the first supplier that meets your needs or offers you the most attention. Pick one that offers you reliable customer service and quality products at competitive prices.

When you survey vendors and request price quotes, don't name a high quantity to take advantage of bulk pricing discounts. Since you don't know how many of your champagne-scented travel candles you will actually sell, stockpiling 5,000 screw-top glass containers that could potentially go unused will negate any savings. Until you are sure that your candle is a seller, your goal should be to spend as little as possible before bringing it to market. Ask your vendor to quote prices at several quantities—be it 50, 100, 200, 500, 1,000, or 5,000—so that you'll have the price breakouts handy for future reference.

Remember that wholesalers will have minimum order requirements, including quantity and dollar amount restrictions. With cost control in mind, purchase the minimum quantity required; hopefully, you can buy a small enough quantity for the purpose of making samples. Be sure to ask what forms of payment they accept; for first-time buyers, prepayment by check, credit card, or COD (Cash on Delivery) is usually required. When you wish to establish credit with a vendor, you will need to provide credit and bank information as well as trade references. If your credit is in good standing, the vendor will likely extend a "net 30" account to you, which allows you 30 days to pay invoices. (See "Getting Paid," page 113, for more information about payment.)

NONTRADITIONAL SOURCING

Some of the best materials don't cost a cent, like seashells from the beach or fallen leaves from a birch tree, or can cost very little, like recycled dishware or vintage bedsheets. When your products rely on these types of materials, you can't guarantee that you'll be able to find them when you need them. You'll probably need to pay close attention to the time of year, rely on making frequent visits to your local thrift store, or use unorthodox gathering methods, like poaching from your mother-in-law's linen closet. When you use nontraditional sources, remember that you should steadily amass a collection of materials. You will never know when a large order is coming your way.

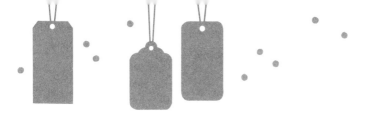

IN FIORE, San Francisco, California
Luxury Holistic Skin Care Products

Working for many years in the fashion industry, Julie Elliott's job required her to travel nearly every week. To deal with this physically and mentally taxing lifestyle, Julie became well acquainted with the art of pampering herself using oils and bathing. Whereas some people do yoga or meditation, Julie created her own rejuvenating beauty ritual that she looked forward to at the end of every day on the road. When she realized that there weren't any companies putting a contemporary and luxurious spin on oils and balms, she quit her job to pursue her interest in holistic skin care. Though it took a while for the concept to catch on, once Julie scored the vociferous support of a glitzy resort, she gained momentum. Julie's products now have a cultish fan base and a celebrity following, making her an indie doyenne in the beauty industry.

How did you learn to make body balms and oils?

When I left my full-time job in 1998, I was in a financial position where I didn't have to work for a while. So I decided to study formulary (how to blend ingredients) and aromatherapy at the Australasian College of Health Sciences. I became amazed at all the different essential oils and carrier oils and their healing properties—how some oils treat skin conditions and which ones are ideal moisturizers. I also became interested in holistic healing modalities, which include anointing with oils to improve health. I emerged from my learning experience with a whole new respect for this field—especially the time-intensive process of distillation. At the time, I realized there wasn't a line of oils and balms on the market that was sophisticated or being shown in a proper light. There were no oils or balms in the luxury market when I started developing In Fiore.

When you launched your company, what types of products did you start with?

I started off with six body oils and three body balms. In my mind, I thought people were going to love the oils and that they wouldn't understand the balms, which is why I began with more oils than balms. But the balm ended up being my most popular product—where my cult following is. In hindsight, it's not surprising, since it took years to perfect the formula for it. I launched a skin care line last year as well—and my sales quadrupled! Apparently, people hem and haw about spending $65 on a body balm but will not hesitate to spend over $300 on facial care.

How do you source materials?

Getting resources is a lot of work. As far as finding raw materials, the Internet and meeting other people in the industry are great for finding distillers, suppliers, and brokers. And then there's a lot that's simply legwork. For example, if you find that sandalwood is from a particular island, you would start researching that island, even if it means going to their Yellow Pages. Whenever you find sources, they become very valuable. They're really worth a lot of money. If you find a really special ingredient, it can become a secret weapon for you.

How did you get your products into stores?

I was the first business to introduce oils and balms into the luxury market—and honestly, people weren't ready for it. When I approached Barneys and Fred Segal, they thought it was interesting, but they were afraid of it. Historically, I don't think these types of products have done well. I was using expensive and rare oils, like jasmine and tuberose. A lot of oil-based products tend to use more commonplace oils—like orange and rosemary—blends that you'd basically see in health food stores. Bacara Resort & Spa in Santa Barbara was my first account. They understood In Fiore. They ordered 5,000 small bottles of oil to use as a hotel amenity. There were many days that my apartment was filled with those little bottles and people helping me. That always seems to be the response to In Fiore: complete resistance or acceptance. When you're introducing something new, there will be a learning curve for buyers, and you have to be steadfast in your vision. You have to be willing to struggle and work with your chin up because there will be a lot of rejection. »

Did you exhibit at any trade shows?

In spring 2001, a friend advised me to do the EXTRACTS Show in New York. The feedback at the show was phenomenal. Beauty editors and people from Estée Lauder and MAC were validating my work. There was no one else doing anything close to what I was doing. I got a lot of really great accounts. The show was great for connections and editorial contacts. I never did EXTRACTS again because I have a very limited and exclusive distribution strategy.

What's your minimum opening order?

$3,500. I used to make a lot of exceptions and allow people to buy below the minimum in the early days because I wanted the exposure, but it becomes problematic later on. I think the days of letting buyers cherry-pick your line have changed. Buyers need to be confident in their choices and buy entire lines because presentation matters. They have to be excited about your work and get their staff excited as well.

So did Fred Segal or Barneys come around eventually?

Fred Segal totally came around, but Barneys didn't. Fred Segal has been an incredible partnership. They have a great team that's interested in nurturing a niche brand. They want you to succeed and have been forthcoming with accounts—forwarding my business to other shops. I don't think I would get this response from a department store. And, truly, your relationships with your retailers should be partnerships. Retailers should make a commitment to your company and promote you. So you really need to find a retailer or shop where your products will thrive.

What is the process of getting product liability insurance for a body product?

You have to submit formulas with testing. The amount of insurance is based on volume of your product, or how many people are using it. It's absolutely essential to have in this field.

How much of what you make do you do yourself?

I partner with a manufacturer of organic products, who of course signs a confidentiality agreement. It's not machine-made; I think that would change the energy of the product. And I have an apprentice who helps me with the body balms. Since skin care is not my forte, I had a manufacturer help me formulate the products.

Buying Equipment

In the beginning, you should keep overhead low and steer clear of making hefty investments in equipment, whether a band saw or a laptop. Over time you can purchase these items as needed. Many community art centers offer open studios that allow artists access to expensive machinery, like a blowtorch or a potter's wheel. You'll know when it's time to invest in your own equipment. Hogging the drying racks with your vases and ticking off those waiting to fire their mugs are both telltale signs you've outgrown the local ceramic studio. Certainly, if efficiency is suffering and orders are piling up, getting your own equipment may be necessary. Still, look for ways to save money, such as splitting the cost of a new kiln with another ceramist or buying a used kiln. The places to look for equipment vary widely: the Internet is a good resource, as are the classified sections of local art and trade newspapers, forums, and Web sites.

The Manufacturing Life

Now that your craft is a business, production will be the lifeline of your company. In the beginning, it's likely that you will be doing a majority of the manufacturing yourself, so devise ways to streamline your process in order to efficiently increase production. Start by breaking the process into smaller sets of tasks, and then find ways to simplify each task. Soon you'll have your production down to a mini-assembly line. Though this may take away from the romantic handmade spirit, ultimately you'll be happier getting your product to your client in a timely manner.

If you're the type that eschews help of any kind, that can be a crimp in your business, especially if Anthropologie decides they want a passel of your checkbook cozies in each of their stores nationwide. Completing that order will be just one of the things on your to-do list, in addition to the minutiae of administrative tasks. This type of situation could realistically occur; you need to be ready with a plan if it does. More than likely, it will be physically impossible to make everything yourself in a timely manner.

As you formulate your production plan, divide the work into that which can only be done by a skilled crafter and that which can be performed by less skilled helpers, like your friends or family, and divide the work accordingly. Some items may need to be outsourced partially, or even completely, and you shouldn't be scrambling to find someone to hire when that day arrives. If you think you might need to hire sewers who can finish a quilt from start to finish, you should have a list of sewers ready to accept orders at a moment's notice. Have them make samples for you before you give them an order; you want to know they can accurately re-create your products for you. Strive for product uniformity throughout. You can't fulfill a wedding invitation order with half looking like they were handmade by a professional and the other half looking like someone's little brother put them together.

TIPS FOR EFFICIENT PRODUCTION

- Learn your craft well to maximize your working speed.
- Set quotas for yourself.
- Find the most efficient procedure to complete your product.
- Create an assembly line and arrange production steps in sequential order.
- Have your tools and materials handy and in one location to avoid moving around too much while you're producing.
- Organize your work space
- Batch your tasks—don't make products one-by-one.

Internationally Made

Because of the high cost of producing goods locally, or in order to support global artisans, some designers seek manufacturers on an international level. One way to find a prospective company is to contact a nonprofit organization, such as Aid to Artisans, that can connect you with crafts-people seeking to maintain their traditions. Visit an international sourcing Web site (see "Internet Resources" on page 156) to search for a company that manufactures products similar to the ones you want to create. Once found, you'll want to send them an e-mail with an image of your product and a description of your production needs. But when you are corresponding with a company halfway around the globe, and one that may not be 100 percent fluent in your language, it can be worrisome. First and foremost, you don't know how legitimate the business or manner of operation really is. Have they really been in business since 1967? Are those photographs on their Web site really from their plant in Shanghai? Will eight-year-old children be hand-beading your evening purses? Will they close up shop tomorrow and run off with your money?

A better way to find global manufacturers is to attend a trade show. You should look for out-of-the-country vendors and inquire if they can produce custom designs. There are even trade shows that specifically showcase international sources (see "Internet Resources"). You can view the quality of their samples and speak to a live person, giving you assurance that this company actually exists. You can ask about development costs to produce a sample and inquire about minimum production quantities. When you're calculating the cost to manufacture your goods, don't forget to factor in additional freight and customs charges. If you worry about the working conditions of the people making your goods, plan to visit the villages or factories (these travel costs can be written off come tax time).

Pricing Your Products

Pricing isn't always about following a formula. Placing a price tag on an object is about creating a perceived value. You may think that what consumers want is low prices. Not always. Price in craft goods often serves as an indication of artistic value and craftsmanship. Furthermore, people aspire to good taste and acquire a sense of status, prestige, and

> ### Placing a price tag on an object is about creating a perceived value.

confidence through material possessions. Price is often an indicator of these things. Now, that doesn't mean you should bestow a four-digit price tag on your three-inch handblown glass bottles, because people can see when a good is overpriced. And not all buyers will take into account how much time it took you to obsessively twist each colored glass. Buyers might compare your goods to comparable machine-made or imported items, but don't price your work lower to try to compete with these types of products; you'll never win. Underpricing your goods can make your product seem inferior or less attractive.

Many new creative-business owners fall victim to their own mis-understandings about price, underselling their goods at bargain prices. Oftentimes, they feel guilty about the profit margin, or they're just thrilled that someone has actually purchased their stuff. Buyers have preconceived ideas of how much an item should cost, so it's up to you to find a happy medium—weighing what people *would* pay for that item against what you think people *should* pay for it. Ultimately, the value you place on the product should warrant the price tag. Sometimes you may be asked to explain your prices, but you should never apologize for them. As best you can, inform the customer about the values of your product (e.g., the fine craftsmanship, uniqueness, and durability), but, mostly, your product should speak for itself.

PRICING GLOSSARY

◉ *Materials cost* is the cost of each material directly used to make the product, including its packaging.

◉ *Labor cost* is the cost of work to manufacture a product. If you have hired help, this cost will include your employees' wages and any added benefits. You have to figure out how much your time is worth when you labor on these goods and how long it takes to make the goods. Our idea of how much our time is worth is usually inflated, so giving yourself a high hourly rate will only give you unrealistic pricing. Find out what studio rates are like for your particular craft.

◉ *Overhead cost* is everything other than labor cost or materials cost; it includes studio costs, selling and promotional expenses (like your trade show booth and advertising), tools, and equipment.

◉ *Profit* is what you've made after you've paid all your expenses.

◉ *Markup* is a percentage of the materials and/or labor cost that is added to reach a price.

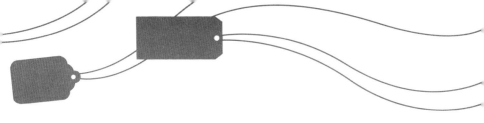

LOVELY DESIGN, Vancouver, British Columbia
Found Paper Stationery

In 1999, Sharilyn Wright, the patron saint of found paper, found herself with a shelf-breaking collection of vintage paper in her closet, from utilitarian columnar ledgers and unused time cards to lined newsprint pads and paper placemats. Something had to be done, so with DIY fervor, she made journals for her friends. What started as holiday presents turned into unexpected marketing materials when the journals fell into some influential hands, including those of a shop owner who wanted her to make more, many more. Much as her products are an insouciant mix of bound paper, Sharilyn's career is a series of exquisite accidents all strung together.

Your designs rely on a fluctuating material source: found paper. It's not like you can just call up a vendor and ask for it. Are you the last stop for friends before they reach the Salvation Army? How much of a challenge is it to collect papers?

Yes, my friends and family are kind enough to bring paper to me sometimes. My husband went on a trip to China and brought back a box of random paper. I was thrilled! I've gotten really good at finding paper. I have to be resourceful and keep my eyes open all the time. I'm always on the lookout, whether it's at someone's place of work or driving down the street and noticing an old printing house.

Your wooden address file is your signature item. How did you come up with the idea for it?

I was searching for the perfect address book for myself—one that would essentially last forever despite having friends move numerous times. I had seen this vintage wire Rolodex that I wanted but couldn't find. Rolodexes in general are pretty bulky and ugly, so I thought about making one out of wood and with my found paper. Thankfully, my dad is a shop teacher, » so I asked him to make me a wooden holder. He made about a dozen or so. Of course, I initially gave them away as gifts.

Your design for your address file is timeless. How popular does it continue to be?

I honestly can't keep up with the demand for them. In the beginning, they used to be made entirely by hand. I mean, I was cutting those tab dividers one by one. I just didn't know any better. I didn't know how to price them, either. I originally charged $34 for them; I was basically giving them away and earning nothing. A store advised me to sell them for more. So now they're up to $75. In the beginning, a lot of designers undervalue their work because they feel guilty charging that much. But it's bad because consumers start wondering why they're so cheap. I think part of the reason people love the address file so much is that it isn't mass-produced. And although it's handmade, it's extremely well-made.

Since you have designs that are proven performers, do you feel the pressure to design more goods?

I do. You have to find a balance. I have a mailing list, so I have to keep people's interest up. I introduce a couple new products every spring or fall, and I switch up the colorways on my existing products every few months. You have to keep it fresh! You also have to offer your customers goods in a variety of prices—mine range from $6 to $75.

Do you do any craft fairs or trade shows?

No, I don't do any. Luckily, stores just seem to contact me. Plus, as I'm already struggling with the demand for my products, bringing them to a trade show would be insane. I wouldn't be able to produce enough. Right now, I tell stores they have to wait between two to six months to receive their order.

How did you finance your business?

I started out small and let things grow. Fortunately, I got a grant from the Canadian government. I applied to this program for people aspiring to be entrepreneurs. It essentially sets you up with mentors, two months' worth of business training, and approximately $2,000 a month for a whole year.

Creating a Pricing Formula

There are as many different ways to create a pricing formula as there are various crafts. The best pricing formula takes into account the cost of materials, labor, and overhead, as well as profit. Some people use materials cost alone and place a markup on that, while others whose labor cost far outshines materials cost (as with needlework) use labor cost alone with a markup. Depending on your craft, you can find a formula that works best for you—it can be as simple or as complicated as you want it to be. The one illustrated below is a markup pricing formula using both materials and labor costs.

Sample

Materials and labor costs for a two-color screen-printed greeting card with envelope.

Materials	Cost	Pricing description
Card Stock	$.05	$27 ream of 250 sheets (2 cards per sheet)
Envelope	$.09	$23 box of 250 envelopes
Ink	$.03	$30 can of ink (enough for 1000 runs)
Clear Plastic Sleeve	$.03	$3 box of 100 sleeves
Labels (outsourced)	$.08	$40 for 500 labels
Labor		
Cutting (outsourced)	$.05	$5 to cut 100 sheets
Scoring (outsourced)	$.08	$8 to score 100 sheets
Printing	$.50	2 hours to print 100 cards ($25/hr for your labor)
Assembly and Packaging	$.38	1 1/2 hours to assemble 100 cards ($25/hr for your labor)
TOTAL	$1.29 for one complete card	

Wholesale Price

(Cost of Materials + Cost of Labor) x Markup = Wholesale Price

$1.29 x 150% markup = $3.22, rounded to $3.25 (This is the wholesale price at which you will sell a single card to retailers.)

As a manufacturer, you will be offering the wholesale price to retailers, who will then resell your products to the end user. Now that you know that materials and labor costs are $1.29 to make one card, you will multiply this amount by a markup to reach the wholesale price. When determining your markup, make sure it is sufficient to include overhead and profit. Here, we added a 50% markup for overhead costs and a 100% markup for profit, which together makes a 150% markup (or wholesale price multiplied by 2.5). At the very minimum, your markup to reach the wholesale price should be 100%, or multiplying by 2. Of course, if you are able to increase your markup, it works to your advantage.

Retail Price

Wholesale Price x Markup = Manufacturer's Suggested Retail Price (MSRP)

$3.25 x 100% markup = $6.50 (This is the retail price that consumers will pay.)

The retail price is the price you will suggest your retailers charge their customers. In general, the standard markup on the wholesale price is 100% (or wholesale price multiplied by 2). For some retailers, the markup can go as high as 150%. It may shock you to hear that retailers take at least 50% of the retail price, but realize that stores have more overhead, advertising, employees, and credit-card processing fees to cover. And remember, too, that when you sell your goods directly to consumers, whether at a craft fair or online, you must offer them at the retail price. Do not undersell the shop owners or online retailers of your goods or else they will stop buying from you. Plus, your profit margin will be bigger when you sell at the retail price!

Evaluating Your Prices

The above formulas set the absolute minimum for your price points so that all parties make a decent profit. However, pricing is a balancing act between what an item actually costs and what your market would be willing to pay for it. This is where the perceived value of your goods comes into play.

You can work backward and price your goods at the retail price you think people would pay for them, then divide that by two to get your wholesale price. For example, considering the craftsmanship and design of your cards, and also considering the going price for cards of this type, you may decide it can be valued at $7.50 (retail).

$7.50 / 2 = $3.75 (This is your new wholesale price. You've just increased your profit margin!)

You could test your prices by selling your jewelry at a sidewalk sale or a craft fair before going public. Once you set a price, you're not married to it, but avoid changing your prices often, if at all. Keeping consistent prices looks more professional and will make your life easier.

If, after you've applied a formula, you find that your retail price point is too high, you might consider cutting the wholesale market out and selling directly to retail. This is not recommended because you'll be cutting out a large segment of potential buyers. Instead of taking this route, consider ways to reduce your product's cost without reducing its salability or integrity. Perhaps remove some time-consuming details or cost-increasing perks— e.g., hang seven charms instead of ten on a bracelet—or shop around for suppliers that offer materials at a lower price point. Another alternative to cutting out wholesale accounts is to create two different product lines: one that you sell exclusively through your Web site and a wholesale line that you produce exclusively for your retailers. For example, your retail line could be a line of quilts handmade by you, while your wholesale line could be completely machine-made by outsourced laborers.

CHAPTER 5

Marketing and
Publicity Strategies

How do you get your hand-felted cloche hat from your home-based studio onto the pages of magazines and into the hands of your target market? By being an active agent of your work! You need to let people know that you exist and that you're making fabulous things. The term "marketing" covers everything you do to get your company on the radar. Business cards, Web sites, free press, and advertisements are all ways of marketing; so is wearing your eye-catching hat about town. As you can see, marketing doesn't necessarily have to put a dent in your wallet. For instance, stirring up "publicity" (also known as public relations or PR), which is getting the media to promote your business for you, can be a relatively inexpensive—often free—marketing method to implement. And you don't have to wait for the media to beat a path to your door. Magazines, newspapers, and Webzines are looking to feature products like yours every day—so be your own publicist and introduce yourself!

Printed Materials

At the base level of marketing are the materials you use to represent your company. Whether you're contacting a local boutique or a magazine, the printed literature you send out communicates a message about your business. Your stationery (including business cards, letterhead, and invoices) should feature your company logo and fit your brand; it should also project professionalism. Business cards, in particular, are like handheld advertisements. People can infer a lot of things from such a small piece of paper through its design and production quality. When possible, you should have these pieces professionally printed so that you're taken seriously.

Catalogs

When you can't show your goods in person, you need to have a printed substitute that gets tongues wagging as effectively. Every designer should have a catalog, or a look-book, with pictures and descriptions of her goods. Catalogs are usually included in your press kit, given out at trade shows, or mailed to prospective retailers. They may change annually, seasonally, or with every trade show, so it's best not to print too many. Typically loaded with photographs of your goods, the catalog should also have a concise description of each product, along with color/size options and item numbers. It's also good to include company history and contact information.

Professionally made catalogs often employ the services of a photographer, a stylist, a graphic designer, and/or a printing press. Cost can easily reach the thousands, and so you may only be able to afford one of these four professionals. If you hire a photographer, he may charge you an hourly fee, and it is not customary for him to arrange your product for the shoot. His sole responsibility is taking the pictures. A photo stylist will arrange your products in a pleasing manner, but she does not necessarily provide the furniture or setting. She merely arranges the items you provide or suggests items to be purchased or rented by you. Good styling is the difference between professionals and amateurs, so if you're not hiring a stylist, practice before the shoot. Once shot, the images are handed over to a graphic designer who will lay them out alongside the text you provide in an attractive, printer-ready format. For any catalog using photographs, the best type of professional printing is four-color.

Prior to even working on a catalog, you should figure out what your needs are. If you'll be sending them to stores that haven't seen your product in person, a fancier presentation with good photographs will be warranted. If you need one just to serve as a reminder at trade shows, your catalog can be a single sheet or card, reproduced at a postcard-printing shop or even on your computer's printer. What you lack in resources, you can make up for with ingenuity and simplicity, so focus on making an uncomplicated, businesslike catalog that retains your style and displays some creativity. If you're not familiar with page-layout programs, you can rely on word processing programs to arrange your catalog.

Getting Professional-Looking Pictures

Your product shots don't need to cost a small fortune. You can find photography students willing to shoot your products at a lesser price in order to build their portfolios, or you can take on the responsibility yourself. With a digital camera and proper lighting, you can take nearly professional-quality photographs. Here are tips for getting great pictures:

❧ Do not use a flash. Flash photography can distort your product's color and details.

❧ Use indirect light. Direct light can create harsh shadows and change the color of your object.

❧ Use soft, diffuse lighting. A photographer's umbrella lighting works well, or you can make your own light box or miniature photography studio with even illumination, using inexpensive clip lamps, PVC piping, a white sheet, and construction paper.

❧ Buy daylight, tungsten, or halogen lightbulbs, not incandescent or fluorescent ones that can make your photographs look yellow or green.

❧ Get to know your camera. Some digital cameras offer manual settings that allow you to change the shutter speed and aperture. Features like macro mode help with focus when you take close-up pictures; a light meter indicates how much light is entering your camera, and the white balance adjusts the colors of your photographs according to lighting conditions.

❧ Use a tripod. Using your hands can make your photos blurry, especially with slow shutter speeds.

❧ Be inventive with your surroundings or use plain backgrounds (like white). If you're using a plain white background, you can curve a piece of poster board to achieve a seamless background.

❧ Take multiple shots and be patient. Reposition your objects, change perspectives, modify your background setting, and try different features on your camera.

❧ Learn Photoshop, or another photo-altering software, so you can make adjustments to your photographs.

Online Presence

The main reason to have a Web site is to connect with your customers and provide them with information about your company and its products. In a world that has become increasingly wired, it's important for every creative business to have a Web site. Although some companies might get along fine without one, a Web site can increase a fledgling company's visibility. Whether you pay a developer to design your site, use a computer program that relies on templates, or custom-design everything from scratch yourself, you can create a site that aptly reflects your company's image. To maximize your Web site's potential as a marketing tool, here are some things to keep in mind:

❧ Use a domain name that isn't too lengthy, is easy to spell, and isn't confusing when said out loud.

❧ Display good photographs of your products.

❧ Update your site frequently with news or new products.

❧ Limit the bells and whistles. They can act as a barrier, slowing the process of connecting your consumers with the information they need.

❧ Offer a mailing list and e-mail periodic newsletters to your subscribing customers.

❧ Include a press page. It looks great when you have a page filled with a list of clippings.

❧ Include a store locator page to direct consumers to retail stores that carry your products.

❧ Include your bio so that your customers can learn about you.

PORT2PORT PRESS, Portland, Maine
Letterpress Stationery

In 2005, Maria Vettese, who lives in Portland, Maine, and her friend Anika Colvin, who lives in Port Townsend, Washington, launched a blog called port2port out of a shared love for photography. Their blog began garnering a regular audience, primarily a community of supportive creatives sharing a mutual admiration for each other's work. When Maria started a solo stationery business called port2port press in 2006, she found herself with an instant audience and customer base, without any press or advertising. What started as a blog to maintain a bicoastal friendship turned into a primary vehicle for attracting customers and making virtual craft friends.

The blog has turned out to be quite successful in generating much of your business. Was that surprising?

It was really surprising when I put my cards out there. The response to it was a little overwhelming, and it was all basically from the blog. I put out a single card design on Etsy (an online marketplace for handmade goods), and it sold out. I put out another card design, and that sold out. I never intended to use the blog to sell things, but it has become my vehicle for showing my latest inspirations and my latest work, and announcing some business news. It was completely accidental. Everything about my business has really happened organically.

Why do you think your blog garners such a regular audience?

Your blog tells a lot about who you are. There are people who naturally gravitate toward us because they like our taste. I think at first it can be hard to put yourself out there in a blog. You have to be willing to share some private information about yourself. »

Unlike other stationery designers, you generate one card design a month. How do you decide what you will design and sell that month?

I started out by selling a single limited-edition card and a set of five cards each month. I produced 100 to 200 of the cards, both for the singles and the sets. Again, it's very organic and just sort of happens. I don't sell singles with regularity anymore, but I do create card sets. I sometimes pull imagery from photographs I've taken. I don't even know what color I will print them in until I put them on the press.

You also have a collaborative line of cards with Natalie Tweedie of Nebo Peklo, an illustrator from Scotland. How did that happen?

We became friends over the blog and designed a line of cards together that feature her gorgeous illustrations. These cards are the only ones I have that are sold in retail shops. It's funny because we've never even met in person!

Your plan is unlike a majority of business plans in that you want to stay small. Is this realistic, and are you starting to feel any pressure to expand and make more money?

I hope to make just enough each month to make me content. It blows my mind already that I am doing this for a living. I was so disillusioned in my 20s! Of course, I do feel some pressure to be bigger or make more money. But I have it in my head right now that all I need to sell is $100 a day, and I'm doing that. So I'm satisfied. Some people don't understand that, for me, it's not all about money—it's about a balance of just enough money and being happy with what I do. How I do business is obviously not for everyone, and even though I have encountered some resistance to my way of thinking, I have eventually enjoyed quite a bit of support from those around me.

What's next for your business or your blog?

As for port2port press, in June of 2006 I launched The Card Society, a unique card-of-the-month club. This is a subscription service where members receive two letterpress-printed cards each month. The response to that has been great so far, and I am really hoping that the membership continues to grow. As for port2port, the blog, Anika and I are about to launch a little online shop on it with lots of cool little things expressing our taste.

Online Communities

Making "friends" over the Internet used to mean meeting questionable characters with equally questionable user IDs in a chat room. Nowadays, it's easier for similar minds to merge by taking part in online communities, like blogs, and social-networking portals, like MySpace.com. The Internet has caused a seismic shift in how goods are marketed by providing these inexpensive opportunities to strengthen your marketing presence. Both of these systems are self-promotional by nature, so they can be used as marketing tools: you can get exposure and create a buzz on a shoestring budget, get validation and feedback on your products, and, best of all, create an initial customer base before launching a business. If you're looking to aggressively promote your business, social-networking portals allow you to post photographs and descriptions of your company and products. You can invite friends and potential customers to your page; these people, in turn, will connect your page to other people, resulting in exponential growth. Some businesses might send invitations one by one, while others might entice people to join their network using gift certificates or free products.

If you're looking to claim more Web real estate with each passing day and to create a more intimate relationship with your audience, blogs are the way to go. Written in diary entry format, with the most recent entry at the top, blogs can reveal many things—from content-driven entries to those that fall into the "too much information" category, like what the blogger had for lunch today. However you choose to use it, your blog can help keep your audience interested in you and returning to you on a daily basis. It can be an effective means of creating publicity, attracting new fans, maintaining existing fans, and getting feedback on your work. On the downside, blogging can be an addictive procrastination device that could take time away from doing more lucrative work.

If blogging appeals to you, there are plenty of ready-made blog hosting sites with attractive templates. You should also sign up for a service that tracks the hits to your site. Most importantly, before you sign up, you must realize that starting a blog is not for the commitment-phobic. Readers often expect a blog post weekly, if not daily. If you don't post frequently, readers may lose interest or think you've abandoned it. You will need to post good content or good pictures. As a craftsperson, you can post your latest inspirations and any finished works. Unlike networking portals, regular readers of blogs often search for authenticity and honesty in postings. If posts are too self-promotional or appear to be a thinly veiled marketing scheme, you may get only cursory visits.

As with any form of social network, both blogs and portals can arouse feelings akin to a high-school popularity contest. In an arena where everyone is competing for attention, popularity is gauged by who's got the most "friends," comments, or "hits." It's easy to get caught up in checking your stats constantly to find out who's reading your blog and in what time zone or continent. It can be disappointing when your stats are low and no one is linking to you or posting comments. One way to increase your visibility is by posting comments on other people's sites, but be sure to leave pertinent comments, not shameless plugs that redirect people to your site. Some blogs also increase visibility by hosting project-oriented activities where others can swap goods or share themed projects such as self-portraits. Above all, when you're not driven by statistics or a need for constant validation, you'll find networking much more enjoyable and blogging much easier to maintain.

BLOG TIPS FROM DESIGN*SPONGE

If creating a blog doesn't sound appealing to you, you can still be a part of the blogging world by reading blogs and posting comments. Or, better yet, you can get your work featured in a high-profile blog. Grace Bonney started her blog, design*sponge (http://designsponge.blogspot.com), in August 2004. Four months later, she was featured in the *New York Times*. An underground phenomenon, she gets an average of 25,000 visits a day. She gets more than three hundred e-mails a day from designers and manufacturers requesting online coverage of their products. Here are her tips for starting a blog or getting your work featured in a high-profile blog:

◦ Find a blog that really fits you. It's not about getting into as many blogs as possible. You should expend your energy on blogs that fit your product well, much in the same way you would target particular stores or magazines for your product. You should get an idea of their tastes and what types of products they show. For example, I do not post anything related to fashion, so don't ask me to post your work if you're a fashion designer.

◦ When you e-mail a blogger, make sure you have some really great photographs of your work or links to images on your Web site. Briefly talk about yourself and your work.

◦ If you want to start your own blog, don't cater to other people's tastes. Start it for yourself and because you believe in it.

* Don't pay attention to the numbers. It's not about how many people visit your blog; it's about connecting with the right audience for your blog, no matter the size. Besides, it can be that one person who visits your blog that makes all the difference. For all you know, your biggest silent fan is an editor at your favorite magazine, or even a celebrity checking you out every day!

Be Your Own Publicist

With most independent designers, there isn't room in the budget for supplies, let alone marketing. Publicity is a good strategy when you're long on time and short on money. But before you attempt to place your products in magazines or online sources, you should realize that getting press mentions is often not about sales, but about raising your company's profile and brand awareness. A press mention is essentially a stamp of approval from an esteemed source. The more visual or written hype you get, the more it solidifies your brand.

You should make a commitment to spend at least a couple hours each week working on your publicity outreach, primarily getting your products in printed media. The grassroots road to getting publicity begins with a trip to your local library or bookstore to make a list of newspapers and magazines that fit your brand and that might be interested in featuring your product. It should be a targeted list, not every magazine and newspaper under the sun. Consider national publications as well as regional

A press mention is essentially a stamp of approval from an esteemed source.

ones. Look through each periodical with an editor's eye and see what section would be most appropriate for your product—maybe it's the "At Home" section of the *Chicago Tribune* or the "Goody Bag" section of *Parents* magazine. Also keep in mind that magazines often have a five-month lead time; if you want to make a suggestion for the holiday gift list, you should send your press kit to them well in advance of the holidays.

In magazines, take note of the names of the market editors. Market editors cover a specific good or market; to find the editor for your specific type of good, turn to the first masthead (list of editors). If there is no market editor listed, take note of the editor for the section where your work fits in and send your press kit to that person instead. At the bottom of the editorial masthead is the address—but be careful not to use the advertising or subscription addresses. If you want to verify the address (perhaps you need a floor or suite number), you can call the publication directly to find out the editor's exact address. While you're on the phone, ask for the editor's e-mail address or find out the e-mail protocol for the magazine. Oftentimes, it's easy to contact editors using standard formats like firstname_lastname@publication.com.

With this information in hand, compose a letter tailored specifically to the editor. Though you'll probably use a similar format for every letter, don't get lazy and send out a generic mass-mailing or an overtly fill-in-the-blanks letter: "Dear [editor], I think my [niche product] would be great in [magazine]." Editors want to see that you've actually taken the time to craft your correspondence and assemble a package specifically for them. It's not necessary to write an ultra-formal letter: be comfortable, concise, and interesting. In your letter, talk a little bit about your company and demonstrate that you've actually read their publication by explaining why your product would be a good fit. Editors are looking for a tear in the fabric of averageness—so explain why your product would be worthy of press coverage.

Editors want to see that you've actually taken the time to craft your correspondence and assemble a package specifically for them.

If an editor likes your work, she'll contact you to ask for more information, samples, or images. Writers and editors are busy people, so don't take it personally if you don't hear from them right away. Do follow up if you haven't received a response after one month. After all, publications rely on designers like you to fill their pages with content, so don't be afraid to speak to them. You should also be prepared to receive requests from freelance writers or editors who are working under tight deadlines and need items from you in a hurry. Consider sending them to a media-friendly Web page inaccessible to your general browsing public; this page can have press releases, fact sheets, and high-resolution photographs that can be downloaded instantly as needed. It's much more convenient and quicker than putting together a sloppy press kit and overnighting the package. If you make your press contact's job easier, they'll be impressed and probably come back to you again in the future. And nothing can serve your company better than developing relationships with the press.

Press Kits

There will be numerous opportunities to express your creative sensibilities in your business—your press kit is one of them. The standard ingredients of a press kit include a catalog with clear photos and descriptions, a line sheet with product numbers and wholesale prices, a biography (sometimes with a photograph) of the company owners, color copies of press clippings, press releases, and product samples (if you can spare them). However, Melissa Davis of Ruby Press PR advises that in the gift, fashion, or lifestyle industry, it is often unnecessary to include press releases. "Editors for these markets are far more visual and are often more interested in what your product looks like than reading about it in a press release. You should only include press releases if you are announcing something that is newsworthy. Otherwise, you can just make a simple fact sheet to accompany your products if you want to discuss them at greater length."

Dare to be imaginative, so that your press kit stands out rather than gets tossed out. But like everything else in the design world, there are good ways to be imaginative, and there are bad ways. If you design a package that is overly clever, with too many bells and whistles, you will run the risk of making it cumbersome or confusing, and your message could be lost. An interplay between creativity and simplicity is always good. Whatever path you choose, you should stay conscious of these design considerations:

❀ Put your contact information on the bottom of every sheet in the press kit.

❀ Be creative in a way that reflects your brand. Reinforce your color motifs or employ your product in the design of your kit (e.g., make a folder using wrapping paper you designed).

❀ Aside from samples, the press kit materials should remain flat. Editors often keep a stack of these press kits on their desk. If you ship your press kit in a cylindrical tube, inevitably the press kit will roll right into an editor's wastebasket.

❀ Don't include too many loose, small items that could fall out of your press kit. As a precaution, you can label each item in case it gets separated from the package.

SENDING SAMPLES

If you send unsolicited samples to publications, it is unlikely that they will be returned to you. These samples are usually considered gifts. However, if an editor requests a press kit along with a sample of a specific item, most of the time they will return it. Be sure to follow up on the item if you don't get it back in a timely manner.

Hiring a Publicist

If you don't have the time or energy to be your own publicist, you can hire one. Publicists are equal parts cheerleader and mentor—singing your praises to the press as well as consulting with you on every facet of your company. They will let you know if your line is stylistically focused, ensure that your catalog is editorially friendly, and review your Web site for branding consistency. Perhaps most importantly, they will develop a marketing strategy and present your company to editors they have relationships with.

Before you hire a publicist, you should make sure you're in the position to create new lines nearly every season so that your future publicist always has something new to present to her contacts. Your company must also be prepared for widespread national recognition, which will cause more sales and production. Another major consideration before hiring a publicist is whether your company is ready to afford one. The cost of a publicist can be equivalent to hiring a full-time employee; you're paying to take advantage of their expertise and their contacts in the media. Publicists work on a monthly retainer, which can run from $1,000 a month for a less experienced firm to upward of $5,000 a month for an established agency. In addition to a publicist's monthly fee, other charges you may incur include telephone, copying, faxing, postage, and shipping fees. Publicists do not design or put together your press kit. They can consult with you on what to include and how it should look, but they are not graphic designers. They also don't help you with advertising. However, they can write the copy for your bio or draft a press release.

You should choose a publicist you have good rapport with, and one who can best represent your company. Store owners and other designers are good resources for finding names of publicists; oftentimes they will list their PR contact on their Web sites. When you hire a publicist, you should put in writing what your expectations are. For example, your publicist should be in regular contact with you to keep you apprised of new developments, such as sample requests from magazines, press mentions, or a list of media that received your press kit.

Store owners and other designers are good resources for finding names of publicists.

Publicists are selective about their clientele. They are looking for easy-to-work-with clients whose talent they believe in and who will uphold or strengthen the reputation of their firm. Most established publicists require you to work with them for a minimum period of time, usually one year. Most prefer not to work on a per-month basis, for good reason. If you work with a publicist for only two months, that may be just enough time for them to send out a handful of press kits. With magazines' long lead times, you'll want your publicist to be around to follow up on those kits and promote your company. There is a cumulative effect to press, so you'll often see your publicist's best work once press for your company starts snowballing.

Reaching for the Stars

For some creative-business owners, getting Sarah Jessica to don their duds is the ultimate dream. Having a celebrity photographed carrying your evening purse at the Emmys or buying your skin care line at Fred Segal can propel a tiny designer into pseudo-rock-star status. If courting celebrities is an important part of your marketing plan, don't bother contacting stars directly unless you have an actual, real-life personal connection. Your samples will go home with the star's manager's dog walker. Instead, participate in a gifting suite, where you pay to offer your wares to the stars. Before award shows and film festivals, PR firms (many of which are Los Angeles–based) host gift lounges in posh hotel suites or swank mansions for celebrities, stylists, and the press.

In exchange for free stuff, celebrities are asked to take pictures holding or wearing the products. PR firms hire photographers and then allow magazine editors to pick through the images they've taken. Although photographs may occasionally make it onto the pages of tabloid magazines, the biggest perk for you is being able to use these pictures as a marketing tool (on your Web site, for example). However, anonymous stylists often shop on behalf of their celebrity clients, so you may not get that face-time you were hoping for with Leonardo. For the most part, gifting is a matter of planting seeds and increasing exposure for your product. But if you're lucky, a sitcom costumer will pick up a collection of your earrings and put them on a show's main character.

These days the "celebrity" label is bestowed upon a broad group of people from A-listers to X-listers, so before you work with a PR firm, ask them for a list of celebrities who have shown up at their previous gifting suites. You should also consider which events fit your brand and target market: a hand-painted belt buckle is appropriate for the MTV Movie Awards, whereas bejeweled bags better match the Golden Globes. Obviously, not everyone's product is fit for a star-studded event, and the hosting PR firms screen carefully. If you are selected, the base fee normally starts around $5,000. In addition to the fee, you will need to give away about a hundred of your hot accessories and pay for travel expenses in order to man your booth. It can be quite costly, and there are no guarantees.

Advertising

Like a press mention, advertising creates awareness and can enhance your company's image, but you'll have to pay to communicate this message to your target market. On the upside, advertising is a quick way to generate sales and leads. There are many places to put an ad: Web site banners, magazines, and newspapers, to name a few. If you're interested in placing an ad in a magazine, select one that fits your target audience, and be sure to look into circulation numbers. If you want to get into a national magazine, for budget reasons you should focus on getting free press first and advertising second. With a single-page ad in a high-circulation magazine often costing as much as a midsize sedan, independent designers' ads are often relegated to the more affordable marketplace at the back of the magazine. Even still, a tiny ad can easily run over $1,000.

In order to be effective, your advertisements need to be well-designed with an emphasis on your brand. If you are going to spend a couple thousand on the ad, it's worth the extra money to hire a graphic designer to create a visually attractive ad. To get your ad the best response possible, pick a good issue for placement. For example, if you are in the gift industry, choose the holiday season issue, or if you are in the wedding industry, choose a month when brides are typically setting plans, like late fall. If you see purchasing rhythms in your business, pick advertising months accordingly.

Creating a Marketing Plan

Perhaps you'll get a taste of fame with an article in *Sunset* magazine or over a thousand Web site hits from a post on a high-profile blog, but eventually that magazine will be off the newsstand and that post will be buried in archives. You will need to think ahead to the next six to ten months and ask yourself how you can keep the momentum going—a successful marketing program is based on frequency. You have to constantly keep your company in your audience's face until they recognize your brand and, eventually, buy your product.

PR is not a marketing method for the impatient.

Before you devise a marketing plan or create any marketing materials, you should have a clear understanding of your target market. Get to know your customers—how they spend, where they hang out, which magazines they read, and what blogs they've got bookmarked—so you can create images and use language that they'll respond to. This information will make your marketing dollars more effective. Knowing your customers' specific desires will also help you create new products that meet their needs.

As you put together a plan, you will need to assess your needs, goals, and budget. If you have immediate marketing needs and want to stir up interest in your business quickly, you can start off with advertising or getting into a high-traffic blog. However, if your marketing budget is tight and you've got the time, then you should put your energy into generating publicity. You will need to cultivate perseverance—sending new materials to editors, following up with them, and reminding them about your company until they bite. PR is not a marketing method for the impatient. You can spend days sending out press kits and not get any responses— and if you do get a response, it might take months for the article to appear. Remember that not everything is appropriate for PR. Your trunk show sale is probably not newsworthy, so don't bother pitching it to local newspapers. Before you implement any of the methods presented in this chapter, you should carefully weigh the appropriateness of one strategy over another.

CHAPTER 6

Making Sales and Order Fulfillment

As a craftsperson, you have many avenues to get your products on the market: you can sell directly to customers at a craft fair or through your Web site, find a shop to take your goods on consignment, hawk your goods at a trade show, or hire a representative to push your products on your behalf. Whatever method you choose to turn your products into cash, remember that selling is more than just moving your inventory. It's about having a positive interaction with your buying public in order to build a customer base that is excited whenever you release a new product, that checks your Web site on a regular basis, and that returns to you at every trade show or craft fair. And remember that a sale isn't a done deal because you have the order form in hand. Your reputation largely hinges on order fulfillment, or your ability to deliver your products satisfactorily in a timely manner, and the quality of your customer service. Every customer interaction you'll have can build up or chip away at your company's reputation.

Craft Fair Revival

In this era of mass production and mass consumption, it's something of a radical statement to pick up a thimble and thread and engage in crafting on your own terms. More and more people are taking this stand, and nothing evidences this change in the zeitgeist more than the revival of craft fairs. Long typecast as old-fashioned and grandmotherly, craft fairs are now lively gathering spots in hipster and punk cultures. Gone are the dried flowers and gift baskets; here to stay are the knitting needles and glue guns. Although the folks behind the craft fair revival are largely in their 20s and 30s, their audience reaches beyond those generations.

Craft fairs are an introduction to the retail market for many creative-business owners. With a "meet, greet, and compete" spirit, they're not just about selling but about congregating with other creative minds to exchange ideas and techniques. Craft fairs are a great arena for new sellers to test their prices and goods in the market, get feedback and reactions from clients and peers, acquire ideas for products and booth displays, and practice customer service skills. Craft fairs range in size from small events held monthly to large craft fairs that travel to various cities nationwide. Entry fees and attendance numbers are commensurate with the size of the fair. As always, it's best to do some research before signing up, to see if the fair lives up to the hype, if it's a good fit for your products, and how comfortable you would feel selling in that environment. (See the "Internet Resources" section on page 156 for a list of nationwide craft fairs.)

A substantial amount of cutting, sewing, or gluing is required months in advance of a fair. If it's your first craft fair, it's hard to know exactly how much product to bring, especially if you've never crafted in quantity. Ask the organizers of the fair for their input. Naturally, you will be limited by time and money—making as much inventory as you can afford or have the time to make. (Plus, you'll have to make sure all the goods fit comfortably in your vehicle so they arrive undamaged at the destination.) As you participate in more craft fairs, you'll learn how much to bring. But until you have that experience to rely on, a good rule of thumb is to bring too much inventory rather than too little. If it's a holiday fair that lasts all weekend, plan to make a lot of goods. In general, you should aim to sell half of what you bring to a fair—not everything. And make more of the items that you think will draw customers to your table.

Remember that most people attending craft fairs aren't looking for a specific item. They're searching for something that catches their eye or speaks to them—something that is cute, cool, or unusual. You will need to prime your goods to be picked, so spruce up your table and make it enticing and approachable. You might want to whip up a tablecloth or hand-paint a sign with your logo. How you merchandise your goods is everything, so keep it clean, uncluttered, and simple, with obvious pricing. If it's your first time doing a show, practice putting together your booth on your dining table, instead of throwing it all in your car and figuring it out on the spot. Consider displaying props so that people know how to use your products—if you made an unusual wine rack, put some bottles in it. It's also good to have your wares in plain sight and at different eye levels, so consider using risers to elevate small items. Try not to stack items so high that they become overwhelming to search through. Lastly, since customers shop better when there is an ample selection of goods, whenever someone purchases an item, you should replenish the stock. You never want your table to run out of inventory.

You'll also need to decide what forms of payment you will accept. If you want to accept cash, consider including the sales tax in your prices to avoid the inconvenience of computing it and providing change in coins. Of course, be sure to bring plenty of small bills for change. And to avoid the confusion of whether the customer had given you a twenty or a ten, put payment in the cash box only after you've provided change. If you choose to take checks, know that this leaves you susceptible to fraudulent purchases. As a line of defense, you should ask for identification and write the customer's driver's-license number and telephone number on the check. And under no circumstance should you allow customers to write a check larger than the total amount, then provide them with change. To circumvent the hassles of cash or potential check fraud, credit cards are your next option. (See "Getting Paid," page 113, for information on accepting credit cards.)

Additional craft fair tips:

Keep track of your expenses, including gas, hotel, and meals (for tax deduction purposes).

Set a sales objective to make at least two, three, or even ten times the total expenses you incur. »

Keep a record of your inventory before and after the sale.

Keep a record of each sale with a good description of the product, or use code numbers.

Be wary of dishonest customers, especially with small items like jewelry. Tie down jewelry so that it can only be removed when purchased.

Don't hold items for anyone unless they've already been purchased.

For outdoor events, be mindful of the effects of the elements (especially wind or sunlight) on your products.

Bring an assistant pair of hands to help package or wrap purchases, and to allow you to make short jaunts to other booths, go to the restroom, or have lunch. It's also helpful if that person is friendly and outgoing.

Have fun and meet people!

Questions to ask when signing up for a craft fair:

- Is it an indoor or outdoor show?
- What items will be provided? What items do I need to bring?
- Will I have access to electrical outlets?
- Will I have access to wi-fi?
- How convenient is parking? Is there a charge for parking?
- Do I have to be accepted to join the show, or is it first come, first served?
- What are the sales and attendance figures for the show?
- How much merchandise should I bring to the show?
- How many exhibitors will be there?
- Who will my neighbors be? Can I choose them?
- Will there be an ATM available? (If not, be prepared to accept checks or credit cards.)

Craft fair checklist (some of these items may be provided; check with the event coordinator):

○ Table, tablecloth, and chairs

○ Tent

○ Display (mannequins, risers, mirrors)

○ Resale permit and business license

○ Business cards or postcards

○ Signage (including a sign with sales policies)

○ Extra price tags

○ Mailing list sign-up sheet

○ Receipt books and a calculator

○ Cash box, credit card terminal, or imprinter

○ Pens and notepaper

○ Packaging material (for delicate goods) and shopping bags

○ Aprons with pockets

○ Twine, masking tape, Scotch tape, duct tape, and scissors

○ Tools of your craft

○ Snacks, drinks, and a cooler

○ Garbage bags

CUSTOM ORDERS

Occasionally, you'll get a buyer who digs your block-printed greeting card but wants to transform it into a baby announcement. Before beginning any custom work, you should provide your customer with a quote and outline your services in writing, stating things like how many proofs or revisions are included and which costs, like shipping, are additional. The quote should also specify that a custom order is nonreturnable and nonrefundable. You should always request half of the total payment up front, to cover materials costs and design expenses in case the buyer doesn't follow through. And you should never promise something you can't deliver!

Consignment

Consignment—placing your goods in a shop, yet retaining legal ownership—is a precursor to setting up a wholesale account with a retailer. The shop essentially acts almost like a sales representative—receiving a commission on each sale, anywhere from 25% to 50% of the total retail price. Usually there is some flexibility, so bargain for a percentage in your favor. Consignment works to the benefit of both designer and shop owner. Shops with limited buying capital are able to offer a large range of goods and test a product's salability before buying it outright. Likewise, designers can test-market their products before offering them in larger wholesale quantities while increasing their retail exposure.

However, you'll need to exercise caution when consigning your goods. Be especially wary if it's a distant store that you can't often visit in person. It is essential that you have a consignment agreement with the store that outlines, at the minimum, how and when you get paid (monthly or quarterly) and who pays for shipping costs. Oftentimes, consignment shops expect you to absorb all or some of the shipping expenses. Make sure you also get a list of items sold when you receive payment. If you are unsure of the shop, start off with a few goods until the buyer has won your trust. If you are considering working with a store on consignment, here are good questions to ask:

❧ How long has the store been in business? If the store is brand new and hasn't earned a reputation among designers yet, be very careful.

❧ What percentage of the store's goods is on consignment and what percentage is being bought outright? If most of their goods are purchased outright, you should encourage the buyer to buy your goods at wholesale instead of consignment.

❧ What are the names of other designers whose goods are on consignment? Contact these designers for their opinions of the shop.

❧ Does their insurance policy cover consigned goods? If your goods are stolen or ruined, will they repay you for them?

❧ How long will they keep your product on their shelves? And if they cannot be sold in that time period, how will they be returned? You don't want stores to keep your items unsold on their shelves too long, as they may become shopworn and therefore difficult to resell.

Wholesale System Necessities

The word "wholesale" connotes someone buying a commodity in bulk at a reduced price. But "bulk" can mean anything from 6 items to 10,000 items or more. If you are interested in going wholesale, what does that mean to you? Do you want to get into a handful of local boutiques nationwide, or are you looking to make a dent in markets dominated by big-name brands? Whatever your goal, you'll need to get hip to the protocol and lingo, as well as prepare forms and set policies, before you join the wholesale game.

Resale Tax Form

You will need to create a resale tax form to get the seller's permit number from anyone who makes a wholesale purchase from you, as proof that their purchases are nontaxable. If you are audited, you will have to provide resale forms for all of your wholesale customers. Follow the template below to create your own.

Sample form

RESALE CERTIFICATE

....
NAME OF PURCHASER

....
ADDRESS OF PURCHASER

I do hereby certify that I hold a valid seller's permit, number .... ,
*and that the tangible personal property described herein, which I shall
purchase from [your business], is purchased for resale. The property to
be purchased for resale is* ....

....
SIGNATURE   TITLE   DATE

Line Sheets

A line sheet displays the names, item numbers, and prices of your products. Pricing can be displayed as MSRP or wholesale. Just be clear about it. If you show the MSRP, you have to let buyers know the percent of their wholesale markdown. Line sheets should also include contact information and sales and delivery policies, such as terms (see "Terms," facing page), minimum order requirements, lead time, and shipping costs.

Minimums

There are two types of minimum order requirements you should set for your products: a minimum dollar amount for opening orders and reorders, and a minimum purchase quantity per good. The minimum opening order will vary depending on your products; it could be as low as $100 or as high as $4,000. The minimum quantity requirement will tell buyers that they need to purchase, say, at least six note cards in any particular design or at least five pillow cushions in a single design. In the beginning, it might be good to set your minimums low to encourage retailers to take a chance on you. Also, a lower minimum opening order will allow smaller shops to purchase from you.

There are several reasons to maintain minimums: to ensure a floor for purchases, to make stores commit to your product, and to prevent buyers from making personal purchases. Be confident in the minimums you set; if a buyer truly wants your product, they will adhere to your requirements.

Order Forms

An order form allows you to take orders from your retailers easily. Your order form should have fields for the buyer's name, company information, terms (see "Terms," facing page), and the all-important purchase order (P.O.) number. Large companies cannot pay for an order unless there is an associated P.O. number, which guarantees that the purchase is authorized. You can sometimes combine the order form and line sheet into one form.

Terms

When retailers ask, "What are your terms?" they mean your payment policy. Terms define how you expect to be paid, especially by new accounts. Typically, before a buyer has established trust and credit with your company, first-time orders should be COD (Cash on Delivery) or prepaid via check or credit card (prepayment is sometimes referred to as "pro forma"). When you're working with established customers who have paid reliably in the past or passed a credit check, you can offer net 30 terms, which allow buyers 30 days from receipt of order to pay for the items. (See "Getting Paid," page 113, for more information.)

Lead Time and Shipping

When buyers place an order, you will have to advise them when they can expect to receive their order. Calculate your lead time according to how long it takes to make or package your items. In general, manufacturers typically give a four-to-six-week lead time to ship trade show orders. You will also need to tell your buyer how the items will ship, as well as the cost.

Return Policy

When you sell your goods to retailers at the wholesale level, they are buying your goods outright. However, most businesses allow their buyers to return or exchange goods within a certain period, provided the goods are returned in salable condition. If you do custom orders, those are not normally returnable. Be clear about this policy in your line sheet.

Other Policies

You can invent policies covering everything from order cancellations to how to sell your goods properly, but these policies can only be enforced when they are stated up front. With regard to how your merchandise is sold, even though retail shops technically own your merchandise and can do what they want with your products—including lowering the price—you can still exert some control by clearly enunciating policies. For instance, you can establish a policy that prevents retailers from selling your product below a certain price point. If you do not like the way your retailer is selling or merchandising your goods, you can attempt to retrieve your items. Policies don't have to be solely restrictive, either—they can be promotional. For example, you can create a policy that encourages bulk orders by offering a small discount on all orders over a certain quantity.

POPPI, Alexandria, Virginia

Jewelry Designer

With a degree in craft and sculpture from Virginia Commonwealth University, Dawn Benedetto never intended to work with beads. To her, beads were for hobbyists. She was knee-deep in making one-of-a-kind sculptural jewelry of molten metal when she got a birthday present that changed her career path. It was merely beads on an elastic string. She played with it and became obsessed with trying to figure out how to anchor and wrap it around her finger. After some serious hours of tinkering, she realized she had crafted a fascinating ring with an elastic band that accommodated a range of ring sizes. She took it to the Buyers Market of American Craft in Philadelphia, and the ring became an instant hit.

There is quite a cult following behind your jewelry; how do you respond to that?

I'm totally flattered that I have groupies! Sometimes people come to my studio in old-town Alexandria covered in my rings. It's flattering and a little freaky. The funny thing is I don't even wear jewelry.

What is it like having product that is so popular?

I'm grateful that Poppi rings really appeal to a wide range of people and that I have good sales numbers. But when you have a business, your life becomes very lopsided. I don't have a lot of time for anyone else but Poppi. And when I do have a free moment, I feel guilty.

How did you go about setting $800 as your minimum opening order?

In the beginning, the minimum order requirement was a lot lower. I increased it after I noticed a pattern in buyers' spending. When buyers would place an opening order around $300, they would hardly ever reorder. But stores that placed an opening order starting around $700 would always reorder. It became clear to me that Poppi rings sell much better when there's more on display. A $400 opening order, which is like ten rings, just doesn't do them justice. They look like they've been picked over. So I realized that stores need to commit to my product and that volume creates a presence in the store. My minimum became 24 pieces, or an $800 opening order minimum. I didn't even bother setting a minimum reorder amount because my buyers already know from experience that the rings sell better when they have more in stock.

What trade shows do you participate in?

I do the New York International Gift Fair twice a year and the Philadelphia Buyers Market of American Craft.

What steps have you taken to protect your work? And have you been knocked off?

In this business, you need to have a lawyer. I hired a patent attorney to file a patent for my designs. I did two design patents, each costing me about $3,500, and a utility patent, which was about $7,800. It took nearly two years to grant the patent. It's expensive, but you have to protect your work. I also filed copyrights for my work.

Yes, I have been knocked off, and it's horrible. Luckily, I think people can tell the difference. I'm a pretty moral person, and it's okay to be inspired by something, but it's not okay to literally knock off someone. I have gone after other designers with a lawyer and most of them have stopped.

Getting Paid

The wholesale business is a relationship of give and take: you've delivered the order, now it's time to collect payment. If only the relationship operated as smoothly as that. As we mentioned in the "Terms" section on page 111, there are several payment plans you can extend to your buyers on wholesale purchases: credit card, COD, or net 30. Credit card or COD payments are standard for opening orders, but for most wholesale buyers, the eventual goal is to open a net 30 account with you, which essentially makes you a credit lender to your retailers—some of which may even be retail giants. In this section, we'll discuss the fine details of each type of payment plan, as well as how to efficiently collect outstanding debt.

Invoices

To turn your inventory into cash, you need to send your retailers a businesslike invoice—essentially a list of goods they've ordered, along with a total sum due. Invoices are usually not included with shipments, but mailed separately. Other pertinent information to include are the date, invoice number (sequentially numbered), your company name (including whom to make the payment out to), mailing address, and phone and fax numbers. Two vital pieces of information that must be on all invoices are the terms of payment, dictating when you need to be paid, and the buyer's purchase order number. If the order was prepaid by credit card or check, make a note of it on the invoice.

It helps to include the word "invoice" in large, bold letters to announce its status as a bill. To encourage your retailers to pay early or on time, you can offer them a small discount if they do so, or you can note that daily interest will be charged (usually a small amount like 1.5%) if their invoice becomes overdue. Whatever your policy, just be sure to print it on the invoice.

Credit Cards

Buyers often appreciate the convenience of being able to use credit cards for purchases. Business owners appreciate the immediacy of the payment and the quick deposit into their bank account. But, of course, there are costs associated with this ease of payment, such as discount, authorization, chargeback, and monthly fees. Luckily, you can be spared equipment costs since companies like PayPal and many merchant card processors offer programs that allow you to process credit cards through your computer. But if you are taking your show on the road, you may need to buy or lease a credit card terminal or buy an old-fashioned imprinter. See what your needs are before committing to any equipment.

To accept credit cards, you will need to set up an account through your bank or a merchant card processor. Shop around to see who's got the most competitive rates, as they can vary wildly from processor to processor. Keep in mind that it's often possible to negotiate and reduce any fees. Your credit and your company's financial activities will be reviewed before approving your account.

When you accept credit cards, maintain good records of sales in case you get a disputed charge from a cardholder. The onus will be on you to prove to the credit card company that the charge is valid. In retail disputes, you'll have to show an original invoice and shipping documents, along with proof of signature and anything else you have to support your claim. If you cannot provide ample evidence, your processor will withdraw the amount from your account along with a chargeback fee, which can run $15 or more.

Cash on Delivery (COD)

COD allows the buyer to pay at the time of delivery. Once an item has been shipped, you'll need to let the buyer know that the shipment is in transit so he can prepare a check. It is up to you to notify both your client and the shipping company if you prefer a cashier's check or a business check. Upon delivery, the buyer will give the check to the shipping driver. The shipping company will then send the payment to you. A downside to COD orders is that a buyer may refuse the shipment—maybe they've changed their mind about the order. There is also no guarantee that the check you receive will be drawn on sufficient funds. Ask retailers who want to pay COD to fill out a credit application so you can verify funds in their account before shipping an order.

Net 30 Terms

Getting paid is a much slower process with net 30 arrangements. Ideally, you will send your customer an invoice, and within 30 days they should send you a payment by check. Although the standard is net 30, you can cut it in half, to net 15, to reduce the waiting time. But sometimes you won't be the one that sets the time period. When you work with large retail stores, you will likely have to accept payment according to how their accounting department operates, which may mean working with net 60, or even net 90, terms.

Naturally there is a risk when you extend credit to anyone: you run the risk of not getting paid at all. First and foremost, any buyer to whom you extend a net 30 account must have filled out an application and passed a credit check. To avoid getting bounced checks (and the banking fees associated with them), double-check if your buyer has sufficient monies in their account before you deposit the check. You can often call the bank and provide the account number to verify funds. You can also wait until the beginning of the month, when accounts normally have funds to cover rent and payroll, to deposit the check—but you may not have the time to call in every check you get. If a check bounces, call the store to notify them of the problem. If they don't make good on their plans to reissue payment, you can ask your bank about ways to collect payment (electronically withdrawing bank-to-bank) or you can hire a collections agency (though they take a percentage of the unpaid invoice). You can also establish a policy that authorizes you to charge their credit card on file whenever you receive a bounced check or if they've fallen behind on payments.

Billing can be a struggle; and waiting for checks to arrive in the mail can be nerve-racking. But problems can happen on both sides, where creative businesses are carelessly slow to bill and buyers are slow to pay. So it's up to you to manage the ebb and flow of your company's cash. Mail invoices in a timely manner, and police delinquent accounts by sending reminders and making phone calls. When accounts are late with payments, make sure you hold any open orders until their account is current.

New business owners are often so thrilled to have buyers that they get shy when it comes time to pursue payment. Although chasing payments may seem like dirty work, if you don't manage your collections properly, you could be forced to seek out a loan to keep cash in your account. After all, you still have your own vendors to pay. It's important that you never extend more credit than you can afford, and that you stay on top of your accounts to avoid finding yourself in a cash-flow crunch.

Approaching Stores

Getting goods into retail stores is a big part of a creative-business owner's dream. Retailers, in general, will buy goods from manufacturers (big and small) or importers at wholesale prices and then resell them. Before you graduate to the big time and offer your products to major retailers, a good baby-step is to hawk your goods to local independent stores in your area.

Unfortunately, you can't hit a city in Starbucks fashion and saturate every corner with your goods. So make a list of the top five stores in a local neighborhood that would be appropriate for your products. First, target the shop at the top of your list—even if it seems out of reach—and then work your way down. Stores want to offer their customers the thrill of finding something that can't be bought anywhere nearby, so oftentimes you can only get one store per neighborhood. Of course, if you have a range of products, you can offer your earrings to a fashion boutique and your greeting cards to the stationery shop across the street, since neither the stores nor your products are in direct competition.

Next, you'll want to do some reconnaissance, both virtual and physical— checking out their brick-and-mortar locations and their online presence. You should make a note of the products they carry (especially the competition), product packaging, and price points. On your scouting trip, absolutely do not introduce yourself as a creative-business owner ready to sell your items, unless you enjoy polite smiles, snickers, and icy glares.

An unprofessional approach like this usually ruins any chance of getting an appointment or making a sale. So remember to be stealthy on your first visit.

If the store agrees to meet with you, it means they are interested in getting more information.

When at last you're ready to approach your dream boutique, call to ask for the name of the owner or buyer. Introduce yourself and let them know you will be sending a package for their consideration. Send a personalized package, with a letter requesting an appointment, along with a catalog, line sheet, and any samples you can spare. When your communication is personalized with extra care, it will attract the buyer's attention. If you don't hear back from them within a couple weeks, be sure to follow up with an e-mail or phone call. If the store agrees to meet with you, it means they are interested in getting more information.

On the day of your appointment, be punctual, dress appropriately for a business meeting, and, most important, bring an air of confidence with you. In addition, bring order forms, pens, samples, a catalog, a sales tax form, and a line sheet. If you are meeting during store hours, you can expect a visit punctuated by phone calls and customer inquiries. As the buyer looks at your items, pay attention to feedback (including any non-verbal communication). Do they seem excited about your products? They may even offer valuable suggestions for improving your products or give their opinions on your price points. If the buyer wants to purchase any items, write up the order, discuss your terms, and let them know when the items will be delivered. Once the merchandise is delivered, make sure you send literature about your company to properly educate the staff, and visit your shops to make sure your products are being properly displayed.

Understand that independent shopkeepers are often very prudent about their purchases, so don't be discouraged if they do not purchase anything right away. They will need to consider many factors—how much they want your product, how well it will coexist with other products, what may compete with it, how much room they have on the floor for it, how much their customers will be excited by it, your price point, and where else you are selling the product—before making a commitment to buy. Sometimes your timing might not be right—they may have just finished filing their quarterly income and sales tax and don't have enough cash flow allocated for purchasing goods. It's hard to know, so don't take it personally. If their budget is limited or they are wary about the salability of a particular product, they might be able to take your items on consignment.

After you've approached stores in your area, you can try reaching out to other retailers online or elsewhere in the country. Craft, lifestyle, and shopping magazines feature stores all the time, so spend some time at your local library creating a list. You can also go to other designers' Web sites to see which retailers stock their goods. It feels great when you've amassed a list of stockists (stores that carry your goods), but it doesn't stop there. Be proactive and follow up with them to see how well your goods are selling, and check to see if they need to reorder.

STORE DISPLAYS

As a marketing tool, and to promote the sale of your goods in stores, you can design and offer display mechanisms for your goods. For example, if you require a retailer to buy a minimum of 20 of your notebooks, you can also sell a tabletop display that holds all of them. This encourages your retailer to buy more of your goods in order to keep the display stocked and helps the goods stand out on the store's shelf. Look for generic display items that you can customize.

RENA TOM, Brooklyn, New York

Jewelry Designer and Shop Owner

Rena Tom likes to multitask: as she mans her boutique, her fingers are busy twisting links for a necklace design, while her eye wanders to her laptop—scoping out new designers on her favorite blog. With so much going on, you can't blame Rena for craving a martini at the end of every day. Originally from Sacramento, California, Rena Tom started her eponymous jewelry business in 2003 after a repetitive-stress wrist injury ended her career as a freelance graphic designer. And, as if one full-time career weren't enough, Rena added a second title in 2005: devoted shop owner/curator. With a discerning eye, she handpicks every journal, pillow, bag, or vase lining the shelves of her *objets d'art* store, Rare Device, in Brooklyn, New York.

What was your first line of jewelry like?

I had about 20 styles—mostly necklaces, rings, and earrings. I really didn't know what I was doing. I was still trying to find my creative voice. So I incorporated many different elements into my jewelry. Now, I churn out a collection every year. If there are designs that do particularly well one year, I carry them over to the next year.

How did you first approach stores with your jewelry line?

Approaching stores is the most nerve-racking thing. Promoting myself was terrifying for me! Ironically, I totally approached stores incorrectly, cold-calling and showing up unannounced with my collection in hand. My first store was Ruby Gallery in San Francisco. The owner, Laura, was very nice and gave me advice about my jewelry line and how I should improve it. Thank goodness she also took some of my pieces. It was a great confidence booster. »

Do you participate in craft shows or trade shows?

I did participate in some local craft shows in San Francisco and continue to do them in New York, too. However, I don't do any trade shows. They're really expensive and I would have to produce a large quantity.

How did Rare Device come about?

My husband and I relocated because he got into graduate school in New York. In the beginning, I used to do jewelry out of our apartment, but it was really depressing not having any interaction with people. I talked to my dog a lot! New York has many great tiny shops that inspire me, so I thought it would be great to open a shop. When a retail space opened up in Brooklyn in September 2005, I jumped on it. Being that it's in New York, where press connections are easier to come by, I was lucky to have garnered quite a bit of press early on.

Do you essentially wear all the hats in both your businesses?

Pretty much. I'm a big-time multitasker. When it's slow for my jewelry business, I switch gears and focus more on my shop, and vice versa. I design and manage both Web sites. I take all the photographs of the products. The fact of the matter is that things just don't happen very fast. Luckily, I do have someone who helps out in the shop a couple days a week. But it's hard to find help and pay them properly. It would be nice to hand over the day-to-day elements to someone else so that I could focus on pushing my jewelry more, growing certain parts of the shop's business, or scouting for more objects to include in my store.

How do you find the objects to sell in your shop?

I find so many things online these days. I find them so much faster as well. I'm always looking out for new designers. I don't rely on trade shows too much at all. When you own a shop in Brooklyn, there are plenty of other shops going to the trade shows, too. Although trade shows conveniently showcase these companies under one roof, boutiques are protective about which designers they are stocking, and they'll prevent designers from placing a product in a shop nearby. When I do go to trade shows, I go so that I can meet and chat with a designer. To scout for products in person, I prefer to go to craft fairs like Renegade.

What types of products are you looking for?

I'm looking for objects that are a good fit with everything else in the shop. Modern goods with clean lines, things that are handmade, or objects with cool stories are always a good match for the store. I pay attention to the designer's professionalism, how focused their collection is, and what their packaging looks like. They should love what they're doing and it should show. They should also deliver items when promised.

Do you often get people showing up cold at your shop to show you their goods?

I do. It's funny because I had done that before, too. I feel really bad when people who show up unannounced have traveled a great distance to show me their work. More often than not, I don't pick up anything I've been shown.

What's next for the shop?

I recently had an event in the shop for Lena Corwin, a designer, and I'd like to do more events like that one. Perhaps I'd like to have a mentor relation-ship with my designers and license some of their work to create objects.

Trade Shows

If your goal is to get your sock monkeys into stores nationwide, then exhibiting at a trade show is likely in your future. Most of these shows happen in metropolitan cities—New York, in particular, plays host to many of the big-name shows—in convention centers, halls, or hotels. They often cater to a specific market: jewelry, gift, pet, and the list goes on. Most trade shows are wholesale and for the "trade" only; however, there are some shows, like the Buyers Market of American Craft in Philadelphia, that have a retail component to them. The shows usually last about three to five days, and the week that the show takes place is usually called "market week." Trade shows attract a broad spectrum of retailers, from tiny boutiques to large-scale department stores, who come to see manufacturers, importers, and indie designers like you from around the world with products to sell.

At most trade shows, the smallest booth can easily set you back $1,000 or more. Booths are priced per square foot, and the fee usually covers the bare minimum, like curtains and drayage (bringing your freight to and from your booth). You will not get a table, a chair, or even a garbage can—those are extras. And, before you think about sharing a booth, know that trade shows have strict guidelines, so double-check with show management to see that sharing is okay. Once you receive your booth assignment, don't sign your contract before checking who your neighbors will be and looking up your booth number on the floor plan to see where it's located. When it comes to trade-show real estate, it's all about location, location, location.

As you'll soon find out, the trade-show grind starts long before you set foot in the convention center. Preparing for a trade show takes at least a couple months of planning and forethought. For some pre-show promotion, send postcards, including photographs of your goods and your booth number, to your stockists as well as to potential stores. If it's your first trade show, it might not be best to build up your inventory in anticipation of orders. It can be difficult to know which item will be the most popular. Since your time is precious, you wouldn't want to spend too much time making items that aren't going to sell. It's best to bring your prototype samples to the show and wait to get a response from retailers. But you should have a production plan for every item, in case of orders.

With trade shows packing in several football fields' worth of vendors, you'll want to create a booth that will capture the attention of passing buyers. Designing your booth doesn't need to be an extravagant or expensive undertaking to be effective. You can project your champagne tastes on a beer budget by keeping your booth clean and simple. Your products are the stars of your show; the booth should serve to highlight your products, not upstage them. Furthermore, don't clutter your booth with too many unnecessary design touches, like vases filled with flowers.

When it comes to trade-show real estate, it's all about location, location, location.

The best booths are well-lit, affordable, easy to assemble, portable, and not overdesigned. Since you'll likely be using your booth for multiple shows, it should also be durable and easy to store between shows. And, most important, always closely follow the manual given by show management when designing and setting up your booth.

Next you have to figure out how to schlep all your goods to the show. If the show is far from home, you may need to hire a freight company to ship your goods and booth fixtures to the show and then back home to you. If this sounds too costly or you worry about freighting your samples, you can always rent fixtures from the companies contracted with the show and either ship your samples to your hotel or carry them with you.

When market week arrives, the air in the convention center will be thick with excitement. It's wonderful to get positive feedback on your goods, especially in the form of orders. But don't get so swept away that you misplace your orders; bring a container to hold them and take it home or back to the hotel every night. The last thing you'd want to do is lose an order. It's unbelievably unprofessional to call your buyer to ask them to resend an order. And don't be overzealous taking any order that comes in—be selective about who carries your products. Remember to be realistic about the lead time and the quantities you promise. If you need to, keep a schedule book throughout the show; there is nothing worse than being unable to deliver within your lead time. If you're a self-production person, don't overestimate your ability to rapidly hand-loom a hundred pillows. If you're chasing the big payday, jubilation can quickly turn to dismay when you realize you can't possibly finish them all in the time you've promised.

Wholesale buyers are a different breed than their retail counterparts. They are very interested in the ordering details (like minimums and lead times), some won't look around your booth much, and they don't always buy on the spot, which makes having good printed materials to hand out essential. Usually, exhibitors request that buyers leave behind a business card in exchange for a catalog or line sheet. This is a good way to interact with buyers: making sure no one grabs a handful of your catalogs and keeping track of leads.

Exhibiting at a trade show can be a physically wearisome experience, especially if you're doing it all on your own. From setting up your booth to breaking it down and manning it eight hours a day for four days straight, it's little wonder that most people come home from these shows a twitching heap of exhaustion. Although it may be tempting to skimp on accommodations when you travel to trade shows, we recommend splurging a bit for a convenient hotel. Trade shows often partner with hotels to offer discounted rates, not to mention a free bus service that will shuttle you between your hotel and the show.

It also helps to bring someone to assist in working your booth. Unlike with a craft fair, simply having a friendly and outgoing helper at a trade show isn't going to be enough. You will need to be choosy. This person will be acting on behalf of your company—your reputation and professionalism are at stake. Your helper must know your company and product lines and be able to speak about them as well as you can. At the very least, this person should know your minimum order requirements and your manufacturing lead times. If you don't know anyone you can trust with that responsibility, you should keep it a one-person show. Many vendors simply ask booth neighbors they trust to watch their booths whenever they need to take small breaks.

Participating in a trade show is a serious commitment; before you apply for one, it's best to check it out in person. As you'll soon learn, a trade show is a costly and tiring, albeit exciting, venture. It all adds up: booth costs, shipping and freight, plane tickets, meals, and a hotel room. Thankfully, the expenses can be eclipsed by the perks: opportunities to hobnob with the press, network with other designers, meet with hundreds of buyers, and go home riding high on the multiple-order express—all within a relatively brief period of time.

Trade Show Packing List:

- ○ Invoice/purchase order forms
- ○ Literature (promotional materials)
- ○ Business cards
- ○ Line sheets
- ○ Catalogs or look-books
- ○ Press kits
- ○ Clipboards (for writing orders)
- ○ Calculators
- ○ Pens
- ○ Scheduling book
- ○ Samples
- ○ Display items
- ○ Lint brush
- ○ Folder or box (to hold orders)
- ○ Comfortable shoes
- ○ Garbage can
- ○ Water and snacks
- ○ Cellular phone
- ○ Breath mints
- ○ Toothbrush
- ○ Layered clothing

NEW YORK INTERNATIONAL GIFT FAIR

In the gift industry, the New York International Gift Fair (NYIGF) has a lore rivaling that of the Emerald City; it is sometimes single-handedly responsible for transforming niche brands into household names and connecting unknowns with press beyond their wildest dreams. It is not surprising that this fabulous, fabled event would have a huge surplus of applicants beating down its door. It's not unheard of for people to wait a couple of years to gain acceptance or to be accepted only to be placed on a waiting list for a booth assignment. If you are hoping to get into a popular section, such as "Accent on Design" or "Handmade," the good news is that it isn't determined on a first-come, first-served basis; instead, it is juried twice a year. While you're waiting for an affirmative reply or lingering on the waiting list, you can participate in other regional shows or ask a representative exhibiting at the fair to pick up your line. If you are rejected, feel free to ask the management about their decision.

Once you're accepted into a powerhouse trade show like the NYIGF, you are making an unstated commitment to remain a permanent exhibitor. Show management expects you to participate in both shows yearly (usually one in January and the other in August). With dozens of hopefuls waiting in the wings, you are surely replaceable. So if you snub this fantastic opportunity, you'll have to reapply for entrance. And if you attempt to skip a show without asking for a sabbatical, you might lose the spot in your preferred section or get placed near less-desirable neighbors at the next show.

Carol Sedestrom Ross, show consultant and ex-Director of Craft Marketing for George Little Management, spoke to us candidly about the selection process for the NYIGF. An entrenched craft show pioneer, she was single-handedly responsible for launching the first large-scale wholesale craft shows in the United States, namely the American Craft Council's Rhinebeck Show in 1973 and their Baltimore Show in 1979.

What are you looking for in NYIGF participants?

We look for new and exciting product lines. Since wholesale buyers often like to buy things in collections, we look for clearly defined lines and pricing that accommodates a variety of budgets. If someone has a $1,000 piece, they should also have a $250 piece. »

About three weeks after a show ends, we send out space renewal contracts to the current exhibitors. When they let us know that they will not exhibit in the next show or ask us for a sabbatical, then we know exactly how many spaces we need to fill for the next show. We jury twice a year: once in the fall, around November, for the January/February show, and again in April/May for the August show. The jury reviews all the applications that have been received and "ranks" them via a point score. Exhibitors are selected to exhibit by those scores, the highest scores get the first invitations, etc. If there are more acceptees than open spaces, they go on a waiting list.

Who is on the jury?

The jury is made up of five to six individuals, usually a mix of current exhibitors and buyers from craft shops and museum stores that sell crafts. They review the applications, which consist of photographs of the products to be exhibited, line sheets, catalogs, and any press materials the potential exhibitor has received. They check the prices, making certain they are appropriate for a gift show, and they try to determine capacity. Could this company fill a large order in a timely fashion? While the jury always strives for the most interesting and innovative work, they also look for good business indicators.

Representatives

If you struggle with the gypsy trade-show lifestyle or the door-to-door sales aspect of approaching stores, consider hiring a representative to do most of the legwork for you. The biggest advantage representatives have to offer is the relationship they have with stores—they know the buyers and talk to them on a regular basis. Representatives' responsibilities and coverage vary widely: Some cover a single territory, like the Northern California–San Francisco area, while others cover several territories or even the entire United States. Some have permanent showrooms and do trade shows, while others are strictly road reps who travel to different local shops. Some are part of a large group, some are independent, and some sub-rep for a showroom.

You might be drawn to a national representative, usually a large group with permanent showrooms in key territories throughout the United States. They can represent you in all territories while offering the benefits of working with a single group: you only have to negotiate one contract and send out one payment per month. You can count on national reps to host a large booth at trade shows, usually in a high-traffic, highly visible area. However, since most of their orders originate from these shows, there may be gaps in orders between shows.

There are a few hurdles you'll need to overcome to land yourself a rep.

There are a few drawbacks to hiring a sales representative. They're expensive: You'll be paying yours a 15% to 20% commission—so you should have an ample profit margin on each of your products to cover your rep's cut. Also, most representatives require that you pay them a commission on all orders you get from the territory they cover, even if the order originated from a relationship that was not established by them. So if you make the acquaintance of a store owner in Berkeley who places an order with you, your Northern California representative technically gets a cut of that order, even though he had nothing to do with it. You also have to provide your rep with samples free of charge. Fees you can expect to incur include charges to display your work in their showroom or their booth at a trade show (unless your goods are a main attraction at the booth), and maybe paying additional commission fees whenever gas prices are on the rise (for road reps).

Before you start shopping for a representative, realize that representatives are not usually receptive to brand-new creative businesses. There are a few hurdles you'll need to overcome to land yourself a rep. First, they want to make sure you've done some work to get yourself into stores. They've seen scads of designers come and go; they're looking for a person who takes their business seriously and for a business that will make them money. Since they have established relationships with stores, they are wary of new designers who could come along and damage their reputation with amateur behavior like failing to ship orders on time. Representatives also want to be assured that you are financially capable of paying them on time: typically on the 1st or 15th of every month for all orders that were shipped or paid in the previous month. If you have accounts on net 30, it could take up to 30 days after you've shipped before you get paid, but you'll have to be able to pay your representative whether or not you've received money from your buyer.

When you're ready to take the step, be sure to hire a representative who is a good fit. Look for someone who represents other lines that could comfortably coexist with yours. They, in turn, will not want to pick up a line that competes with lines they already represent. Your rep should be personable and professional, since they will be acting on behalf of your business. You can find representatives at trade shows, permanent showrooms, or even on other designers' Web sites. A good rep believes in your product and will target stores that are perfect for your goods. A rep learns about your line, gets you into stores that could've been hard to get on your own, knows the story behind your company, and can riff on your product like it's the coolest thing on earth.

Once you've found a representative, you will negotiate a contract that covers the relationship: how they will get paid and how much notice they'll need if you want to end the relationship. As with any agreement, it needs to outline your expectations as well. You need to know how many trade shows, if any, they will commit to in a given year. And, to avoid any surprises, they need to inform you of possible fees you could incur.

Being a Good Salesperson

Whether at a craft fair or a trade show, you will be acting as your company's salesperson. Like all other talents, learning to be a good salesperson takes time. If you're shy, you'll have to get over it quickly. Practice at home so it doesn't feel awkward. Luckily, the more you speak to people, the easier it will be. For starters, smile, greet, and make your customers feel important. You should be friendly without being insincere, or else you run the risk of giving off a used-car-salesman scent or a selling-from-the-trunk-of-your-car vibe—instantly transforming yourself from likable to loathsome.

A good salesperson is visible and spirited. Don't just sit behind your table or stare blankly into space until someone enters your booth. You should be alert and attentive all the time. At a trade show, a single person can reward you with your big break; you never know. Don't make assumptions about buyers, either turning your nose up at someone because they're wearing shabby slip-ons or ignoring the little guys to butter up a major department store. If someone looks interested in a product, elaborate on it by offering interesting factoids, such as where the raw materials originated or the source of your inspiration. If you engage every single person in your booth with respect and courtesy and have conversations without pushing a sale, you will get sales.

But sometimes, before you've even opened your mouth, your appearance and demeanor have already spoken for you. Because you never get a second chance to make a first impression, always put your best face forward and dress as a creative professional. This doesn't mean that you should wear a power suit or dress like someone you're not. The type of event will dictate what type of attire is appropriate, but general cleanliness and neatness are always appreciated.

Because you never get a second chance to make a first impression, always put your best face forward and dress as a creative professional.

The first time at a show or fair can make you feel like the success of your business rests on a wing and a prayer. Be ready for praise and rejection—hoping, of course, that anyone with something nasty to say will just pass you by. You know that your goods won't appeal to everyone, so try not to take it personally. If you feel discouraged when people aren't ordering or buying immediately after the doors open, remember that people often need time to walk around the show and digest their environment. And if you notice that people are window-shopping, not buying, don't let it affect your demeanor. You should continue to smile—any display of ill temper could affect your sales. Staying friendly and open to conversation might help you learn more about why people aren't buying: maybe people love your work but can't afford it, or maybe a competitor has a table closer to the front door. Of course, you will inevitably have at least one bad show for one reason or another, but always try to learn from it and enjoy yourself.

Order Fulfillment

Independent businesses have been known to score orders in the tens of thousands from major retailers. On the surface, that dollar figure sounds fantastic, but realize that a sweet order like that is usually accompanied by a hefty tome outlining the buyer's stringent specifications—from where to place a UPC label to how large the shipping boxes should be. Place that UPC label on the right- instead of the left-hand corner and you can be sure the entire order will be returned to you at your expense. Read the store manuals carefully. If a retailer doesn't provide strict guidelines, create some yourself, to decrease the potential for damages or returns.

Your products need to arrive at their destination in good condition, which is often easier said than done.

Don't cut corners on packaging costs. Use stuffing materials such as packing peanuts, air packets, or crumpled paper. Buy quality boxes and good packaging tape. As packing materials can be costly, avoid purchasing any from local shipping retailers or office supply stores. Instead, buy them at wholesale cost from packaging companies or paper distributors. As you package your shipment, assume that the box will be tossed about wildly and stacked below heavier boxes before getting to its destination. Placing a "fragile" sticker on it will do very little to combat rough handling. With that in mind, fill up every square inch of the box to make it resistant to compression and to prevent items inside from shifting. Use filler suitable for the item being shipped: if you are shipping a heavy ceramic pot, opt for Styrofoam rather than paper.

You should also think about protecting your shipments against the elements, especially rain and snow. Even if it's sunny where you live, there might be rain at your package's destination in Seattle. So enclose your pillows in plastic bags if you want them to arrive dry and salable. When you're done, securely tape the entire box.

In order to ship your packages, you will need to buy a scale to properly weigh them, and maybe even an envelope scale for small lightweight shipments. Each box should include a packing slip to help avoid disputes between you and the shop owner about the box's contents. Double-check the recipient's address: If you put the wrong street number, the shipping company will charge you a fee for the mistake. If there are several boxes in a single shipment going to that incorrect address, you will be assessed a fee for every box. For COD orders, make sure you've properly indicated "COD" on every label included in that shipment.

The most popular methods of shipping are UPS, FedEx, and the U.S. Postal Service. You can stick to one company for a majority of shipments or use all three. When you are sending wholesale orders, it's best to use one of the big-name shipping companies because of their online tracking systems and streamlined billing capabilities. These companies can usually pick up from your location so you don't have to drag 50-pound boxes to your local post office. And if you find yourself shipping orders nearly every day, you can even arrange for a daily pickup. Of course, these services come with fees (dependent upon the amount of total shipments a week), and you will be billed on a weekly basis.

No matter which service provider you choose, once you start shipping items in volume, you are bound to run into problems like damaged items, incorrect deliveries, and lost packages. If a package is damaged in transit, you can file a claim with the shipping company. Occasionally, you may have an order so large that you'll need a trucking company; prices for that service will vary based on the goods being shipped, how much they weigh, and their destination. If fulfilling orders becomes so overwhelming that it takes up most of your day, you can consider working with fulfillment houses that can handle warehousing, packing, and distribution.

Customer Service

If you thought being your own boss would be fantastic because you would have no one to report to, you've never been more wrong. Now you will answer to your new bosses: customers, buyers, and members of the press. And with them, your responsiveness is everything; this group can push your business up as easily as they can bring it crashing down. In this age of fast food and same-day service, people prefer quick responses and instant shipments.

People will make judgments about your business based on short interactions at fairs, over the phone, or via e-mail. With every response you make, you are molding your reputation. With overworked and understaffed creative businesses, the tired owner can often become her own worst enemy. If you are slow to answer your e-mails or calls, or don't answer at all, people will think that you're in over your head and taking in more orders than you can handle, that you're too self-important to return e-mails, or, worse yet, that you're just plain incompetent. No matter how talented you are or how popular your company is, you cannot afford to dismiss e-mails or phone calls. Surprise people by responding quickly! Within 24 hours is nice, but try to keep it two to three days maximum, if possible.

And although you are running a business, you don't have to be ultra-formal and businesslike with your relationships. Formality can be boring, putting a wall between you and your customers. People appreciate some human interconnectivity, so start your e-mails with "Hi, Joe" instead of "Dear Mr. Smith." Then again, you shouldn't be too casual or chummy, e.g., explaining that you couldn't ship their order because your son had his championship soccer game yesterday. You also don't want to be emotional if you get into a disagreement. Stay professional at all times, but open the door to having real human conversations—many of these people are your peers, after all. As there are plenty of one-man operations, you don't need to hide behind the faux "we." At the heart of it, no one wants to have a relationship with a faceless company.

CHAPTER 7

Ups, Downs, and
Next Steps

By now you know that running a creative business takes more than creativity—grit and self-discipline count for so much. Sometimes that hard work pays off early, and sometimes it takes years. Once your business reaches that tipping point and becomes more lucrative, many things will likely happen: You'll become more confident. Hiring employees and leasing space outside your home will become a necessity. You may meet and collaborate with other crafters. And you'll come up with design ideas you never thought possible! Of course, there will be some adjustments and curveballs along the way: A company may knock off your designs. You might suffer from burnout. The stork may have a delivery for you. And you may learn lessons the hard way by losing money, time, and, sometimes, friends. Now that you're in the thick of it, here's what you can expect in the months and years ahead.

Knocked Off

For a trailblazing independent designer, nothing is more infuriating than opening up a mail-order catalog to find your product's doppelganger staring back at you for half the price. You've just been knocked off. While it's great to be a source of inspiration, you don't want to be fresh blood for a tired industrial designer. Unfortunately, everything you make can be imitated in one way or another.

Mass-merchandise companies are often behind the most unscrupulous forms of this transgression—making watered-down, mass-produced versions of your handmade goods. They sometimes find targets while trolling through the aisles of a trade show. To add insult to injury, they often place a covert order and use your products as their production samples. Then, there are other independent designers who engage in similar practices, scanning magazines and blogs for ideas ripe for the picking. These designers may resort to plagiarism out of creative envy or even financial pressure in their business. Some don't realize the gravity of the issue, while others simply think no one will notice.

Because of the quick dissemination of visual material these days and the gray areas in intellectual property laws, any work you make accessible to the public is vulnerable to being knocked off. Although it comes with the territory, there are preventive actions you can take. First, as we mentioned previously, you should have protected your work via trademark, copyright, or patent. Consulting with an intellectual property attorney will help you ascertain whether you should engage in a legal war of words or full-fledged battle with the offending company. Some small business owners shy away from any recourse because they feel they don't stand a chance against a retail conglomerate's legal team—much like David taking on Goliath. (Of course, you know how that story ended.)

Aside from taking legal action, you should give yourself a pep talk. Being creatively violated can be a highly emotional experience for a designer. An idea that you've spent months cultivating has just been snatched up and distributed without a cent of a royalty payment. Naturally, it's upsetting when this happens to you, but stay confident in your work and keep your creative wheels spinning. It's important that you not allow embittered feelings to hinder or prevent the release of new work. Remember that you'll always have the creative advantage in this situation because only you have the inside line to your future creative plans. You'll always be ahead of the curve, while the people imitating you will always be steps behind.

Where Are the Orders?

For an indie business owner, there's nothing worse than waking up from a trade show with a $5,000 hangover. Initiation into the world of craft manufacturing can be harsh. If you've put your leather belts and cuffs out there and sales aren't pouring in, what should you do? Give up on your dream? It's easy to feel defeated when the sales numbers don't match your passion. The first thing you should do is analyze the situation: Maybe your product is seasonal and you launched at the wrong time, maybe your prices weren't set appropriately, or maybe you picked the wrong trade show. Or perhaps the problem isn't product-related at all, and what's lacking is a good marketing plan (revisit "Creating a Marketing Plan," page 101).

If you truly believe in your products, be proactive and make some changes. Nothing different will happen unless you do something different. Looking at your product with new eyes, consider changing the tooled patterns on your leather goods from old-school country & western to rockabilly chic—it might make all the difference. Or maybe you need to manipulate the price. Most people's automatic reaction to poorly selling items is to decrease the price. This isn't always the solution; sometimes increasing the price is actually called for. As we discussed in Chapter 4,

If you truly believe in your products, be proactive and make some changes.

watching consumers' responses to prices can be interesting, in a psychological-experiment kind of way. Pricing ties in to a complex system of beliefs that goes beyond affordability to issues such as desire, quality, and branding. The notion of affordability is subjective—the same person who balks at a $200 hand-loomed shawl might splurge on a $400 pair of machine-molded sunglasses. So before you succumb to the knee-jerk reaction to mark down your prices, think about increasing them instead. You might be delightfully surprised to see what unfolds.

Entering this business, you have to be ready to put your talent out there, even anticipating a less-than-sufficient financial return in the beginning. Don't be discouraged if your business is off to a slow start. It takes time, sometimes years, to realize a profit. Some of the designers interviewed for this book were met with cold receptions and doors closed in their faces when they first introduced their goods to potential buyers. When you bring new things to the market that aren't trendy or don't have instant universal appeal, people have a tendency to be afraid at first. If someone tells you "it just isn't done," sometimes that means you should work harder and do it anyway. If you have faith in your creative abilities and believe in what you're selling, the day will come when people wise up and embrace your work wholeheartedly.

LEAN TIMES

Consider the big picture: For the most part, crafts are not necessities. No one really needs a felt button or a cozy of any kind—toaster, iPod, or beer can. Craft items are fun, luxury items. So when the financial climate cools, people may cut down on these nonessentials. But you can still sell crafts in hard times if you shift your focus to products that are more functional or practical or that cater to specific occasions, like weddings or new babies. You should also anticipate lowering the prices of your items. Many craft-based businesses survive through the ups and downs of the economy, and yours can, too.

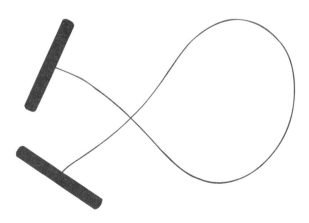

VARIEGATED INC., Hudson, New York
Textiles

Not known for their subtlety, Variegated Inc.—a partnership between Jim Deskevich and Corbett Marshall—entered the home-wares market by introducing pillows and duvets with bold colors and patterns. Their goods' charm is inextricably linked to their attention to craftsmanship. But despite their products receiving a warm welcome in the marketplace, things did not go as smoothly as they hoped. Like any good behind-the-scenes story, they had to hit rock bottom to discover what they really wanted out of their business. Thankfully, their optimistic attitude put a positive spin on a bad sales year: the partners were able to achieve the perspective that helped them regain control of and find fulfillment in their business.

How many of your products are handmade by you?

Corbett: If a pillow or duvet comes out of here, I've probably cut it and Jim's sewn it. If it's screen-printed, we did it here in the studio. We have worked with production houses here in the United States, but it's always difficult and so expensive because a production run of 100 pieces is still considered sampling.

How do you split up your responsibilities?

Jim: Probably not as well as we think we could. We know what we like and don't like to do. Corbett can't stand to be on the phone, so he keeps up the invoicing and housekeeping end while I do a lot of the customer interfacing. However, we share responsibilities in designing and production. There's a constant redefining of responsibilities. You have to be able to turn over complete trust to your partner. In the beginning, it was hard for me to let go of some responsibilities because I'm a little bit of a control freak and I have trouble delegating. »

Corbett: We have a personal and professional life together and the lines are often blurry. We live and work in the same space. At the beginning of the day, we usually have a meeting to set the tasks for the day.

Do you struggle with pricing your goods?

Jim: We put a lot of time and effort into making things people will enjoy. We piece all our items, including duvets, which contain a lot of pieces. Some items can take a full day to make. Because we don't make too many of one item, our production costs go up, both in labor and raw materials. People often don't understand that the pillows we make have to pay for materials, labor, utilities, production losses, and our booth at a trade show. If it costs us $20 to make a pillow, we're going to wholesale it for $40. And then a retail shop marks it up to $80. We'd like to sell things for less, but then we'd be undermining our stores.

Corbett: We want to make beautiful things, but we also have to make a living. Pricing can be agonizing. We like to make things by hand and hope that people appreciate it. Perhaps people think that goods should be less expensive because they think of home decor as disposable. But things don't have to be disposable. Just look at quilts that were made 300 years ago! They were stunning then as they are now.

What was your first experience like at a trade show?

Jim: In the early days of the business, we had a representative who showcased our work along with ten other designers, at the New York International Gift Fair. It was great because we didn't have to come up with the money or booth design and our rep had a booth in the Accent on Design section. Then our rep dropped all their wholesale lines and we had to exhibit at the shows on our own. We started from square one in the Handmade section. At that show, we spent $8,000 but sold only $750 worth of merchandise. We eventually got a booth in Accent on Design and even won an award for our booth design in August 2004.

What type of feedback do you get at trade shows?

Corbett: People really love us or don't get us. We have strong personalities and we put it into our work. For some reason, there will always be buyers that are incredibly rude at the trade shows. I think they feel like they're in this position of power where they can just step into your booth and tell you what they think is wrong with your product, your booth, or even you.

What string of events changed your business in 2005?

Jim: We had a rough fall 2005 season. At the August show, we got a bunch of orders for the holiday season. However, the production houses that were making them fell behind—like eight weeks behind schedule! Since orders weren't getting delivered until the end of November, retailers started canceling their orders. That was a real turning point in our business, when we started to realize that we weren't in charge anymore.

Are you still doing the NYIGF?

Corbett: After the August 2005 show, we decided to take a sabbatical. And recently, we decided to take a chance and drop our tenure from the show—at least for a while. One thing we do miss about the show is the incredible network of friends we've made. When you think you're in it all alone, the shows help you realize that you're not the only one losing sleep and making mistakes.

What changes are you making to your business?

Jim: We're definitely stepping back and looking to control the way our products are sold. Right now, we have a wide distribution, but a lot of the companies on our list are simply buying at the minimum, like four or five pillows or throws. We've let people slide under the minimum because of the pressure to sell to make up for your trade-show costs. Now, we want to have really consistent relationships with our stores and have them show that they are committed to us. We set restrictions now like, if they don't have a bed in their store, then they can't buy any of our duvet sets. We're really restructuring right now and regaining control of our livelihood.

Change is good! And it certainly sounds like a burden's been lifted and you're entering a new and exciting stage in your business with increased clarity. What's next?

Jim: It's kind of strange to say, but I really think we were lucky enough to have a bad sales year. Sometimes hitting bottom can spark immense creativity. It puts you in this crisis situation where you have to react. »

You end up taking the biggest risks when you have nothing to lose. We're at this stage where we feel like we're trying to reestablish ourselves as more than just production artists. We're rebirthing and incubating ideas—and the eggs are about to hatch. We're evaluating our products, expanding lines that are doing well and editing those that aren't. It's really exciting when you get your mojo back.

Corbett: Getting into business is like that playground ride—the merry-go-round ride—that spins around when you push it. When more kids get on, it starts spinning around faster and faster. You want to get off but you're scared. Then you realize that the ride is only six inches off the ground. So you jump! Sure, you've skinned your knee and you're a little dizzy, but now you have a better sense of what to do if you want to get on that ride again.

Burnout

When people start seeing your goods in stores and your face pops up in magazines, it's easy for them to believe that you're spending your days counting your dough poolside. However, the reality for a creative-business owner is usually not as glamorous as it seems: you have less free time than ever, you work around the clock, and your craft, which was once a source of stress relief, is now a principal source of stress. It is often difficult to step away from your job because of the never-ending feeling of being behind. Eventually, the superhero lifestyle will take a physical and mental toll on you. If you're overcome with creative paralysis, stale time wears away at your motivation to work, you feel exhausted and anxious, or you suffer from headaches or unexplained rashes—these are telltale signs that burnout has set in.

It's safe to say that all owners go through a period of burnout. Perhaps you set your goals too ambitiously high and you feel constantly overwhelmed. Or maybe you need to regain balance in your business by spending more time with your fingers on the potter's wheel instead of on the computer's keyboard. Or you need to set boundaries on your workday so that you have more time with your girlfriends. Or maybe you just need a break!

To overcome burnout, you will need to find a way to recapture the fulfillment your business used to provide. Instead of working around the clock and on weekends, acknowledge when you've done an honest day's work and grant yourself some downtime. Find ways to make yourself feel less overwhelmed. When you're responsible for order fulfillment, stock management, accounts payable, accounts receivable, purchasing, press, customer service, design, *and* janitorial services, you need to prioritize, or enlist the help of others to lift some of the burden.

Life in Balance

Enterprising creatives tend to possess the triple personality of multi-tasker/overachiever/control freak. With a constant spate of tasks on their plate, eating real meals and spending quality time with friends sometimes take a backseat to finishing orders and projects. A business can certainly throw your life completely off-balance. Remember to support the people in your life and give yourself days off to get together with your friends for a serious night of getting down. And if you're subsisting on TV dinners, your house is a mess, or you need to shop for the holidays, don't feel guilty about putting your business on hold. To make sure you take time to decompress, take inventory of your life on a monthly basis using this questionnaire:

Health, Well-Being, and Relaxation

Have I been physically active?

Am I getting enough sleep?

Am I eating regular meals?

Am I making an effort to keep up my appearance?

Have I taken a vacation recently?

Have I visited a local museum, restaurant, park, or theater lately?

Have I gotten a massage or gone to the spa lately?

Friends & Family

Am I keeping in touch with my friends and family?

Are there any phone calls or e-mails I need to return?

Am I being supportive of my friends' and family members' endeavors and milestones?

Have I attended events I've been invited to, like graduations, openings, receptions, weddings, or birthdays?

Am I remembering birthdays and anniversaries?

Do I need to send anyone a thank-you note? »

- Am I maintaining my home?
- Am I spending enough quality time with my partner and children?

Business

- Am I caught up with my business's finances? Are all my accounts reconciled on a monthly basis?
- Am I paying my bills on time?
- Do I need to collect payment from any vendors?
- Am I making enough money?
- Is my workplace clean?
- Have I spent several hours this month working on marketing?
- Are there e-mails I need to return?
- Is there anyone in my creative network I should contact?

CREATIVE BLOCK

When you find yourself working more on the day-to-day tasks to keep your business running and much less on the one thing you want to do—create—you may hit a creative slump. It means you've lost the most important part of the design equation: yourself. Devote some time to rejuvenating and reconnecting with yourself. Meditate. Take a nap. Go for a brisk walk. Don't be afraid to walk away from your business for some fresh air or to engage in a short burst of physical activity. If you work primarily from home, change the scenery—walk into another room or, better yet, go to a coffee shop or park. A change of environment can open up creative channels in your mind. Recharging your creativity can be as simple as listening to a different radio station or going on a creative field trip to an international market or a museum. Remember that the process of renewal is important; it allows you to return to your work refreshed and refueled.

Parent Entrepreneurs

The pitter-patter of little feet can often bring an independent business to a screeching halt, or at least a slowdown. Certainly, the way you do business now will drastically change once the stork arrives. Even the most prudent of plans will not completely prepare you for the task of raising a child and running a business at the same time. Although combining your dual joys in life will make life twice as rewarding, it will also make it twice as challenging, since both parts of your life will compete for your time and attention.

Unless you have a business partner, it is unlikely that you'll receive a real maternity or paternity leave, since no one can fully act as your substitute. To prepare for this, you should slow your business's pace while you are still expecting. Take on fewer projects and reduce the number of labor-intensive products you offer, or design new products requiring less handiwork. If you are pregnant, avoid physically taxing events, like trade shows, and try not to work right up to your due date. Don't schedule a lot of work for after the baby's birth either, because it's impossible to know how much you'll be able to handle. If your retailers have outstanding orders from you as the delivery date nears, let them know that you are expecting a child. Many people can sympathize with expecting parents.

It goes without saying that, first and foremost, you will be a parent. You should always take care of your children's needs first. On the other hand, it hardly excuses you from less-than-professional behavior, like delivering your tote bags late to the MOMA or forgetting to file your sales tax returns. The best thing to do is to set routines for both your baby and your workday. Give your child a steady schedule so that he eats, naps, and plays at the same times every day. Predictability works to the benefit of both your child and your business to keep you in control of your day. But if you're having trouble taking care of both business and baby, don't struggle for martyrdom or wear sleep deprivation like a badge of honor— ask your family for help or hire a babysitter or assistant.

People often have the misperception that stay-at-home working parents have it all—the flexibility of owning a business *and* they get to be with their children all day. Your friends may look at you with how-does-she-do-it awe, when the reality is you're not doing it very well at all. Mixing the demands of raising your children with the pressure of running a business can produce a stress-charged cocktail. Suddenly your work space, already doubling as a dining room, has a third identity as a playroom. Answering phone calls is now a dice roll—what are the chances your son will wake up from his nap while you're talking to a buyer? You'll adopt different voices, like a low voice for when your child is sleeping and a trying-to-sound-professional voice while your daughter is making funny faces at you. But it gets easier as your children get older, because you'll have the opportunity to work and play with your kids, all at the same time. Children are very inquisitive and want to do what you do—so you can ask them to help you stuff boxes with packing peanuts or affix labels onto shipments.

Once your child has arrived, all else will diminish in importance. Give yourself a break to adjust and understand your new living situation and get to know your baby. Hibernate. Screen calls. Auto-reply to e-mails. Though having children will definitely bring a new, challenging dimension to your juggling act as a business owner, you'll probably find being in business for yourself a better option than sitting in traffic as you commute to a noncreative daily grind, paying out more than half your salary for day care and professional attire.

Hiring Employees

Over time, your craft may transform into a full-time business in desperate need of more hands than just your own. You may have too many products to manufacture on your own without sacrificing quality, or just too many orders to fill and distribute by yourself. Although work relief might begin by recruiting your husband, dad, sister, or friend, the follies of nepotism will make apparent the need to find more qualified and skilled helpers. But taking the operation to the next level can be a bittersweet decision— on the one hand, you'll get the help you so desperately need, but on the other hand, you also have to pay for it. And even though you will want to hire hardworking, intelligent employees, it might be hard for you to compensate properly. For businesses on a shoestring budget, typical candidates would be interns (a cheap source of talent) or part-time employees for whom you don't need to provide benefits.

Being a small-business owner means doing many tasks yourself, even if you might not be very good at some of them. So you should focus on hiring people for positions where you are weakest or for tasks you find tedious. But before you hire anyone, know what you can afford to pay, what specific skills are required, and what their daily tasks would be. You should also request a cover letter and résumé from your job candidates. Since it's hard to judge by curriculum vitae alone, get a little help from social networking Web sites and prescreen your prospective employee.

You'd be amazed at what people reveal about themselves online—would you want an assistant whose MySpace.com motto is "I'm bossy!"? Probably not. Hold out for the perfect candidate who fits the bill, will work for the amount of money you are offering, and sincerely wants to help your company grow. You have the opportunity to choose whom you will work with, so choose wisely.

While it's great to get help, understand that you have legal responsibilities to your employees, such as providing a safe work environment and giving them breaks. If someone is working at your place of business, you'll need to get worker's compensation insurance in the event that she gets hurt. If she accidentally breaks her leg as she's climbing up your studio's makeshift loft, worker's compensation would cover medical costs, lost wages, and liability should she decide to sue you.

When it comes to the administrative end of paying employees, doing your own payroll, particularly calculating taxes, can be nothing short of nightmarish—you'll have to withhold federal and state taxes, social security, FICA (Federal Insurance Contribution Act), and Medicare. You will also need to file Employer's Federal Quarterly Tax Returns. Unless you're an ultra-DIY business owner who loves to learn about *every* aspect of the business, you should sign up with a payroll company. They'll handle all of your payroll needs plus provide your employees with the tax documents to file their income tax returns.

Opening your business to strangers also means exposing them to any trade secrets you may have. To protect your intellectual property against internal design espionage, you should consider having an attorney draft a nondisclosure agreement (NDA) or a noncompete agreement for your employees to sign. When an employee signs an NDA, they are legally bound to keep any of your business's secret information confidential. It can also forbid them from taking your ideas and using them for personal gain. A noncompete agreement will prohibit your employee from working for one of your direct competitors for a certain time period after they've ceased being your employee.

How to Be a Good Employer and Boss

After doing it all on your own, it will certainly be an adjustment to delegate work and share your space with another person. Being a good employer means you have to clearly define the policies and culture of your company's work life, outlining what you expect and will allow at your place of business. Are pets okay to bring to work? Can employees play music while they work? Is there a dress code? What time does the workday begin? How long are lunch breaks? An employee handbook (even if it is just a single page with bulleted points) should define the work environment and expectations, as well as outline a procedure should your employees have a complaint. Employees should be reviewed periodically, usually after the first three months and annually thereafter, at which time you would assess their performance and how well they adhere to the employee handbook.

For many creative-business owners, taking on the role of "boss" is a very new and often table-turning experience. Being a good boss requires learning appropriate behavior for cultivating a valuable relationship between you and your subordinates. Being a bad boss is bad for business—it stimulates inefficiency, low morale, and eventually turnover. So to prevent your employees from spending their time lamenting about you, here are some tips to achieve proper leadership in the workplace:

❧ No task is below you. Do the same tasks as if you were working alone, including grunge work like taking out the garbage or mopping the floor. It helps to show your employees that you are indeed a part of the team and not merely someone barking orders.

❧ Keep your personal and professional lives separate. Don't let your employees hear you speaking on the phone about your personal problems. Likewise, don't become so chummy with your assistant that she starts letting you in on all her dating woes. You don't want your workdays to turn into therapy sessions. Of course, it's okay to talk about any serious problems your employee has that may impact her job performance.

❧ Project a caring demeanor, but you can't always be nice. You'll sometimes have to do difficult things like restrict lunch breaks that go on too long, turn down vacation requests, and fire unsatisfactory employees.

❧ Don't let small problems grow. If you notice that an employee is spending too much time on personal phone calls, tell that person right away.

❧ Give your employees only work-related responsibilities. If you hired someone to be a graphic designer, don't ask that person to do work not in the original job description, like picking up your laundry from the cleaners.

❧ Keep the business's financial issues to yourself (and your bookkeeper). If your company is going through a period of financial difficulty, don't let your employees know, or else they'll start looking for another job.

❧ Coach your employees. Show respect for their ideas. Praise them in public when they are doing a good job and correct them or provide constructive criticism in private.

JONATHAN ADLER, New York, New York
Potter, Designer

Jonathan Adler's story has all the makings of a modern-day fairy tale: after trading a job in the movie industry for a struggling existence as a potter, Adler quickly found himself a veritable style guru at the helm of a burgeoning design empire. With eponymous stores stretching from Miami Beach to Los Angeles, Adler's success can be attributed to an ability to design products that bring art and design closer together. Under his philosophy of "Happy Chic," every art form has become a fertile area of exploration, allowing him to apply his design principles to goods beyond his wildest dreams, like furniture and even hotels. Adler's larger-than-life personality is captured in everything he designs. Jonathan is a hard-core modernist who isn't afraid of a little kitsch; it's hardly a surprise that his products are destined to be remembered and revered.

In the early years, did you struggle with pricing your goods?

I was a complete idiot and I knew nothing about pricing. When I first started, I got an order from Barneys and I was thrilled! But I was charging $20 for pots that took me a full day to make—so it was a money-losing proposition. But I wouldn't have done it any differently. I'm glad I underpriced myself in the beginning because it enabled me to get some orders, establish relationships with stores, and learn the ropes. Once I had the relationships in place, I was able to increase my prices.

How long did you wear all the hats in your business? When did you start shedding some of them?

For the first few years, I used to get to the studio by 7:00 A.M., throw one hundred mugs, attach all the handles, fire the kiln, pack boxes, do invoices, etc. until 11:00 P.M. That was my life seven days a week! Hiring my first assistant was a revelation. It seemed hard to believe that I could afford » to pay someone. I gradually learned to delegate the tasks that didn't have to be done by *moi*. I hired people to paint, glaze, fire, and pack. And I just concentrated on throwing pots, which is my unique skill. For me, the biggest challenge, both conceptually and practically, was finding somebody to take over the throwing duties. My husband used to tell me all the time that I had to delegate the throwing in order to concentrate on the bigger picture, but I would smugly reply that I had a unique skill and nobody would be able to replicate it. Of course, I was wrong.

Prior to working with Aid to Artisans, what avenues did you explore in search of production relief?

I tried everything. I hired freelance throwers, and each one was more disastrous than the last. I tried outsourcing to domestic manufacturers, who were incredibly expensive and never delivered on their promises. I went to Mexico several times to look at different factories. When I hooked up with Aid to Artisans and checked out the workshop in Peru, I didn't have high hopes. But it all worked out beautifully and I continue to work with my Peruvian workshop to this day.

I love that you have a manifesto on your Web site. Is having a mission statement particularly helpful in the design process to ensure that your work is always charged with your values?

Yes! I think a lot of craftspeople get bogged down in the day-to-day activities of their business and never have a chance to step back and think about the big picture. For me, my manifesto is an expression of my philosophy of design and of life in general. I strive to make stuff that adheres to the ideas and values in my manifesto. For me, the most important thing was thinking of my work in a philosophical way, rather than purely looking at the formal characteristics of my designs. In other words, when I first started I thought of myself as the "striped pottery guy." But then I thought about what the point of my stripey pots was. I realized that I was trying to say a lot with my hand-thrown stripey pots. They were about good design and craftsmanship and modernism, and they were definitely happy, unlike the dour minimalism that was so common. The formal language was stripey pots, but the point of my work was Happy Chic. Suddenly, I realized that I could make improbable leaps in my work and my choice of media (from clay to pillows to furniture to retail design), as long as it all fell under the rubric of Happy Chic.

When you look at my collection, you will see lots of different products and colors and patterns, but I hope that the main thing you see is a consistency of spirit and a lot of beautiful stuff!

Would you say that your recent work is more experimental and expressive of your voice?

I'm very lucky to have my own retail stores. Store buyers can be the enemy of creativity. They often want to play it safe and look to vendors for a predictable commodity, and they like to pigeonhole designers. With my own stores, I have the freedom to make whatever I want, no matter how mad it is, and present it directly to the consumer. The interesting thing is that the more outré and idiosyncratic a piece is—a vase covered in breasts, a giant ceramic VW Beetle, a needlepoint pillow inspired by Liza Minnelli— the more successful it is. I believe that consumers want a break from the predictable, and I'm lucky to have a platform to present my voice.

Do you employ other designers?

I now have a design staff of four people, and we work very collaboratively. Being a craftsperson can be very isolating. My early years were lonely and exhausting. So I feel very lucky to have colleagues to bounce ideas around with and have some giggles.

Considering how busy you are, do you ever wish you could spend more time at the potter's wheel?

No! Having given my pretty years to the wheel, I don't miss it. I think people idealize craftspeople and think there's something noble about spending all your time making stuff. But I found it boring and stressful. When I spend time making stuff in my studio, I'm always working on new ideas instead of doing boring old production.

Looking over your many years in the business, which accomplishment are you most proud of?

I am proud of a lot. I'm proud to have built a company that employs sixty creative people—and to be making stuff that I love! I consider myself very lucky. When I quit my heinous job in the movie business 13 years ago and decided to try making a go of it as a potter, I knew that I was making a » lot of sacrifices. I assumed that I was sacrificing any chances of success, money, fame, or glamour to pursue my passion for clay. I was totally fine with that sacrifice if it meant I would be happy.

When I first started my business, my idea of success was spending my weekends hawking my wares at rain-soaked craft fairs. Just being able to find an audience for my work would have been enough. So, I'm ecstatic to have the unexpected and quite fun design gig I have now and to work with so many great people!

Outgrowing the Home Base

At some point, your business may threaten to burst the confines of your pint-size pad and send you into the streets looking for space. That is a good reason to lease space: when you feel the crunch of progress in your home base—your kitchen is stacked with boxes and packing peanuts, and your closets are spilling over with inventory—or if your lines have expanded so much that you need a showroom to meet with buyers. However, getting a new space because you scored one big order and are anticipating growth, or, worse yet, because it would boost your ego—those are not good reasons. Although it's not necessary to have a brick-and-mortar location these days to be considered a legitimate business, getting a dedicated business space is often an important milestone to achieve—a symbol of success.

If it isn't a vibrant retail haven, your products should be popular enough to pull in destination shoppers.

If you harbor daydreams of occupying a tiny shop-*cum*-studio or talking one-on-one with buyers in a professional office, you should know that the reality of managing a storefront or showroom requires a tremendous amount of work and will reduce the flexibility of your schedule—affording you less time to practice your craft. Of course, there are benefits to operating an exclusive business location: it keeps your home and business life separate, and it can showcase your business and brand. If you open a retail storefront, you'll have the ability to test new products and develop merchandising methods.

Picking a retail location requires analyzing the amount of foot traffic in the area. If it isn't a vibrant retail haven, your products should be popular enough to pull in destination shoppers. You'll also have to set a regular schedule so that your customers know when to stop by, which sometimes means having evening and weekend shop hours. If you work alone, you might have to hire someone to staff the shop. Similar to keeping your Web site fresh, you'll have to update the products and displays in your shop because new and surprising merchandise displays are what attracts repeat business.

Before you go out on your own, you might want to test the waters by partnering with a co-op retailer in your area, if you can find one. Co-op retailers allow you to be part of the retail experience in an alternative way by renting out space in their shop, where you can place your full line of goods on a consignment basis. In addition, they also request that you work in the shop, which means you get to see what it's like to interact with customers, test-market new products, and get feedback and advice from other designers.

Whatever you decide is appropriate for your business—a store, showroom, studio, or office—you should be in a position where your schedule allows for it and, most important, where your sales can support the additional expense. You should always put your business's best interests ahead of your own, so set a budget you can stick to. Commercial leases are often negotiable, so if the property managers truly want your business, they may accommodate you at a lower cost. If most spaces are still beyond your budget, you should consider alternative arrangements, like sharing a studio space with another craftsperson.

Before you hit the pavement hunting for vacant spaces, ask yourself:

❧ What is the purpose of this space—day-to-day business operations, production work, order fulfillment, wholesale showroom, and/or retail space?

❧ What type of amenities do I need—Internet connection, utility sink, windows to allow natural light?

❧ What is the minimum square footage I require?

❧ Is the location convenient for my employees and me?

When reviewing a potential space and lease agreement, ask the property manager these questions:

❧ What is included in the rent? Are utilities included?

❧ Is the space accessible for deliveries and pickups?

❧ Will zoning laws allow me to run my business in the space?

How long is the lease agreement? Can I get a month-to-month lease?

Can I paint or decorate the space?

Is there additional storage space?

What is the parking situation like if I need to drive or if I am expecting visitors?

What are the bathrooms like?

Am I required to get insurance?

What is the foot traffic like in the neighborhood?

Calling It Quits

It's good to have a determined attitude as your business cruises along, but you'll also need to be willing to accept failure as a real possibility. The path to making a successful business is hardly straightforward and the payoff is not often immediate. Even a thriving business may have a limited life span as your interests or trends change. And not everyone is cut out for the dual role of entrepreneur and professional crafter. If you find yourself spending too much time handcrafting your products and becoming emotionally attached to them, you might not be suited for a role as manufacturer. As unglamorous as that title is and as label-resistant as you may be, in this business, that is what you are.

So whether by slow or swift decline, sometimes even good things must come to an end. You'll know when it's time to move on. But first, give yourself props for taking the courage to elevate your craft beyond hobby status. Your next steps are entirely up to you. There is absolutely no shame in going back to a 9-to-5 gig. Realize that if you started your business straight out of college and don't have any "real world" working experience, you'll probably have to start with an entry-level position. Employers may not understand self-starters, so be sure your résumé reflects the skills you've developed. Perhaps you will leave your business because it has opened new career doors that build on your crafting experience: You could teach your craft, write a book, or have your own column in a craft magazine. You could leave this creative sphere for an even better one that has all of the excitement, paired with a steady paycheck.

COLLABORATIVE PROJECTS

To take your work to a different level, sometimes it takes blending your hand with another person's. Collaboration allows you to step away from your usual hyper-individualistic process to discover a new avenue of artistic expression combining two or more points of view. Collaboration doesn't have to be limited to working with someone in your field, either: very interesting things can happen when two different specialties come together—like what would happen if a quilter and jewelry designer joined forces?

If you want to proposition someone for a collaborative project, you should be ready to be a part of a team and to relinquish sole ownership of ideas. Early on, it should be made clear if all parties will act as equals or if one party will be heading the project. Everyone involved will need to be dedicated and motivated to follow through with the project. Since this is a business as well, you will also have to figure out how the product will be made, marketed, and sold and how tasks, expenses, and profits will be divided. To do all this, a constant flow of communication will be essential. With excellent rapport and organization, this joint effort could turn into a pseudo-partnership, not to mention a long-lasting friendship.

With technology these days, you can essentially coproduce a project with anyone across the globe. Finding a potential collaborator is often pretty easy—the person's name is already in your mind. It's someone whose work you admire! Maybe it's another craft peer, or perhaps it's a pioneer in your field. Take, for example, the independent pottery design team KleinReid (James Klein and David Reid) in Brooklyn, New York: With an it-doesn't-hurt-to-ask attitude, they headed straight for the top and approached the grand doyenne of pottery for a collaborative project. They were longtime devotees of Eva Zeisel, a living legend and premier industrial designer of the 20th century, and the thought of working with her was a fantastic notion. But to their surprise and delight, she agreed to collaborate with them. Over several years, they've blended their individual styles into a unified expression, even exploring other mediums beyond clay—like printmaking. It just goes to show that you shouldn't be afraid to dream big.

Growing Your Business

You have a lot to be proud of, namely building your business from the ground up. But as you grow your business, everything else will grow with it—your bills, your orders, and your fans! But just because you've graduated from new kid on the block to crafter du jour, don't be too quick to rest on your laurels, thinking you've hit the big time. Entrepreneurship is very Darwinian; stagnancy will hurt you, and fame can be fleeting if you don't keep at it. Your goal should be to grow your business steadily, at a manageable pace that generates a steady stream of income. Only regularly launching new products and remaining in the public eye with an ongoing marketing program can accomplish this.

Growing your business means steadily fixing and improving your internal business practices—and really analyzing each problem area so you can properly fix it. Business owners often think that beefing up marketing is the solution for most problems. It isn't. If your cash flow is continually low, don't be too quick to launch a new marketing program to increase revenue—maybe fixing your accounts-receivable practices would be the proper solution. And if you need to increase revenue, instead of marketing, you may just need to hire more production help.

Regardless of how seasoned you are as an independent craftsperson, there are always new levels to reach and new markets to cover. Consider creating versions of your products that cater to different markets or niche groups. Think of offshoot projects to open up other streams of income, particularly opportunities to earn money without putting in much labor or energy, like entering into licensing agreements with companies that can mass-produce your designs. If you're keen on writing, pen a how-to book or write articles for your favorite craft magazine. If speaking is more your forte, keep an eye out for potential crafty television gigs and teaching workshops to establish a platform for your expertise.

> **Regardless of how seasoned you are as an independent craftsperson, there are always new levels to reach and new markets to cover.**

Your business will go through changes; one minute you'll be doing one thing and, before you know it, you'll be ricocheting down another path. Of course, as an artist, it's okay to recognize when your art or aesthetic has found a new perch from which to fly. However, as a businessperson, try not to make drastic changes to your company's overall identity too often, if at all. All your marketing efforts are aimed at getting people to recognize your company—change the look of it too quickly or too frequently and you'll destroy any branding progress you've made. Consistency is key.

Truly, there is no universal algorithm to make your creative dream continuously successful. Every creative business will ride through highs, lows, and various stages of profitability and creativity. Some of the highs, like getting an e-mail from a fan in Tokyo, will totally surprise you, while some of the lows, like receiving a $10,000 order return because the zippers were faulty, will absolutely break your heart. For small businesses, every experience holds a lesson. Through it all, remember that only you can define what success is for your business—maybe it's your bottom line, maybe it's fame, or maybe it's simply the feeling of gratification that comes from producing work based on your creativity.

Internet Resources

For more information on the interviewees featured in the book:

Beth Weintraub, *www.bethweintraub.com*
Blissen, *www.blissen.com*
Denyse Schmidt, *www.dsquilts.com*
Design*Sponge, *www.designsponge.blogspot.com*
In Fiore, *www.infiore.net*
Jill Bliss, *www.jillbliss.com*
Jonathan Adler, *www.jonathanadler.com*
KleinReid, *www.kleinreid.com*
Lotta Jansdotter, *www.jansdotter.com*
Lovely Design, *www.lovelydesign.com*
Poppi, *www.poppishop.com*
port2port press, *www.port2portpress.com*
Rare Device, *www.raredevice.net*
Rena Tom, *www.renatom.com*
Ruby PR, *www.rubypr.com*
Sunshine's Scarves, *www.sunshinescarves.com*
Variegated, Inc, *www.variegatedinc.com*
Wool & Hoop, *www.woolandhoop.com*

Craft Fairs

Art vs. Craft, *www.artvscraft.com*
Bazaar Bizarre, *www.bazaarbizarre.org*
Craftland, *www.craftlandshow.com*
Handmade Arcade, *www.handmadearcade.com*
Maker Faire, *www.makezine.com/faire*
Renegade Craft Fair, *www.renegadecraft.com*
Urban Craft Uprising, *www.urbancraftuprising.com*

Social Portals and Blog Hosts

Blogger, *www.blogger.com*
LiveJournal, *www.livejournal.com*
MySpace, *www.myspace.com*
TypePad, *www.typepad.com*
Word Press, *www.wordpress.com*

Craft Forums & Communities

Craft Mafia, *www.craftmafia.com*
Craft Revolution, *www.craftrevolution.com*
CraftSanity, *www.craftsanity.com*
Craftster, *www.craftster.org*
CraftyPod, *www.craftypod.wordpress.com*
Etsy, *www.etsy.com*
Get Crafty, *www.getcrafty.com*
Supernaturale, *www.supernaturale.com*
The Switchboards, *www.theswitchboards.com*
Whip Up, *www.whipup.net*

Trade Shows

American Craft Council Baltimore Show, *www.craftcouncil.org/baltimore*
California Market Center, *www.californiamarketcenter.com*
Craft & Hobby Association, *www.chashow.com*
EXTRACTS, *www.extractsny.com*
George Little Management, *www.glmshows.com*
International Contemporary Furniture Fair, *www.icff.com*
International Gem & Jewelry Show, *www.intergem.com*
New York International Gift Fair, *www.nyigf.com*
Philadelphia Buyers Market of American Craft, *www.americancraft.com/BMAC*
Sources LA, *www.sourcesla.com*

Craft Guilds & Organizations

American Craft Council, *www.craftcouncil.org*
Handcrafted Soap Makers Guild, *www.soapguild.org*
Jeweler's Resource Bureau, *www.jewelersresource.com*

Outsourcing

Aid to Artisans, *www.aidtoartisans.org*
Alibaba, *www.alibaba.com*

Protecting Your Work

Copysentry, *www.copysentry.com*
Creative Commons, *www.creativecommons.com*
Nolo Press, *www.nolo.com*
U.S. Copyright Office, *www.copyright.gov*
U.S. Trademark Office, *www.uspto.gov*

U. S. Government Resources

U.S. Small Business Administration, *www.sba.gov*
Internal Revenue Service, *www.irs.gov*
U.S. Equal Employment Opportunity Commission, *www.eeoc.gov*

Index

Acknowledgments

To my editor, Lisa Campbell, for her guidance, patience, humor, and belief in this project. To my agent, Lilly Ghahremani, for keeping me on track and motivating me with pep talks. A special thank-you goes to Anh-Minh Le for her research assistance. This project was a huge learning experience and would not have been possible without the contributions made by Lotta Anderson, Jill Bliss, Joy Durham, Jonathan Adler, Katherine Shaughnessy, Julie Elliott, Sharilyn Wright, Maria Vettese, Melissa Davis, Dawn Benedetto, Rena Tom, Grace Bonney, Carol Sedestrom Ross, Beth Weintraub, Denyse Schmidt, Jim Deskevich, Corbett Marshall, Kelly Sperbeck, David Reid, Leah Kramer, Carolina Graber, Marie Kare, Alli Kim-Czerniak, Lena Corwin, Whitney Smith, Mark Smithvithias, and Kari Feinstein. Thank you all for taking the time out of your tight schedules to share your knowledge and experiences with me.

To my family—my husband, Marvin; my mom, Dely; my dad, Alfonso; and my mother-in-law, Minda—thank you especially for your support and for keeping the kids occupied so I could finish this book. And to my proudest creations, my kids, Lauryn and Miles, for being inspirations in my life and work.